COOKING FOR

A healthy and varied diet which reflects the latest research into foods best suited to the treatment of diabetes.

COOKING FOR DIABETES

by

JILL METCALFE

Cookware for photography kindly loaned
by Harrods and Boots Cookshop

Illustrated by Kim Blundell

THORSONS PUBLISHERS LIMITED
Wellingborough, Northamptonshire

First published 1985

British Library Cataloguing in Publication Data

Metcalfe, Jill
    Cooking for diabetes.
    1. Diabetes — Diet therapy — Recipes
    I. Title
    641.5'6314   RC662

ISBN 0-7225-1152-3

Printed and bound in Great Britain

ACKNOWLEDGEMENTS

To Mets — for love, spelling and washing up and to
Kate for her nimble fingers on the typewriter.

CONTENTS

PREFACE

While I hope that the ideas in this book will be sought after because they represent the best dietary approach to the management of the diabetic condition, it is more important that they convince the reader that following or catering for a 'special' diet is not limiting, time consuming or expensive — indeed not that 'special' at all!

JILL METCALFE

INTRODUCTION: What Is Diabetes?

The title of this chapter may appear a little superfluous, after all you have probably picked up this book because you have diabetes, or have become involved through a member of the family or a friend who has the disorder. Nevertheless information on diabetes is constantly increasing and changing, explanations given nowadays are very different from what they were, so a short introduction will not go amiss.

Diabetes — What Do We Mean?

Diabetes (diabetes mellitus) is a name given to a disorder which is characterized by a raised level of glucose in the blood. Glucose is the simplest form of sugar, being the ultimate breakdown product of the carbohydrate foods (starches and sugars) that we eat. Everyone has some glucose in the blood, as it is needed as an immediate source of energy. In non-diabetics the level of glucose, regardless of the amount of food eaten (to provide glucose), or the amount of activity undertaken (to use up glucose), never exceeds 8mmols per litre (150mg per 100ml), and never drops below 2mmols per litre (35mg per 100ml). Diabetes is diagnosed if the level of glucose in the blood, when no food has been eaten, exceeds 8mmols per litre (150mg per 100ml).

What Causes the High Blood Glucose?

If non-diabetics can eat and exercise as much as they like without getting 'highs' or 'lows' in blood glucose, what has gone wrong in the diabetic? It is that the vital hormone **insulin** (which is produced in the pancreas) is either absent or in insufficient quantities for the body's needs. If there is no insulin present at all, then daily insulin injections will be required, usually once, twice or more a day, or in a few individuals, provided continuously via an insulin pump. Where there is some insulin available, more care in the choice and amount of food eaten may be sufficient to match the supply with demand. Where the supply is still not adequate then hypoglycaemic tablets (which increase the efficiency, and in some cases, production of insulin) may achieve adequate control.

How Does Insulin Work?

It is clear that if the level of glucose in the blood goes up when there is insufficient insulin available, then a function of insulin must be to control the amount of glucose in the blood. We get all the energy we need for our body to work and for our activities, from the food we eat. We cannot make use of the energy in food until it is broken down into its simplest forms. As we have said, glucose is the breakdown product from the sugary and starchy foods (carbohydrate) that we eat. However, we cannot use this energy (in the form of blood glucose) until it has been carried from the blood into the actual cells of the body. Here it is used up (metabolized) in a fascinating and complex energy releasing process. It is in the carrying of the glucose from the blood into the cells that insulin is so important. If you imagine insulin as a tube train, glucose as the commuters, the home station as the blood, and the destination station as the cells, you will see that without the tube train (the insulin) the passengers (the glucose) can't get from their homes (the blood) to their destination stations (the cells) and work. Similar analogies in various forms are very frequently used by doctors, nurses and dietitians in explaining how insulin is the important 'key' that enables energy (from the food we eat) to be used.

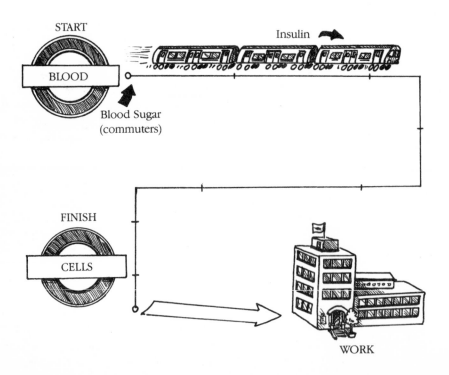

START

Insulin

BLOOD

Blood Sugar
(commuters)

FINISH

CELLS

WORK

Is There a Big Difference Between Having No Insulin or Not Enough?

If there is no insulin available, then the body very rapidly fails to function and unless insulin is provided the individual will die. For this reason, the two scientists who are most widely credited with making insulin available to humans, Banting and Best, are recognized as truly historic 'life savers'.

If there is some, but insufficient, insulin, deterioration is that much slower. In many cases, with suitable adjustments of diet, the level of glucose in the blood can be maintained within near normal limits. In one group, overweight diabetics, it is not a case of reduced supplies of insulin; if anything, more insulin than normal is circulating. However, it appears that the body is resistant to the insulin's action (just as if somebody had changed the lock so the insulin key doesn't fit) and in this group, weight loss, which reduces the resistance, is essential if control is to be achieved.

Insulin has roles to play other than carrying glucose into the cells, it controls the storage of energy in the form of glycogen, controls the fat stores (both their deposition and mobilization) in the body and is important in the process by which the body builds up protein for growth and repair. Obviously if insulin is lacking, all these processes fail, which explains why in diabetics with grossly inadequate insulin supplies, significant weight loss occurs despite what appears to be an adequate diet. When the body recognizes that energy is not being made available from the breakdown of the carbohydrate that is eaten, it turns to the fat and protein stores and tries to use these instead. This produces toxic waste products which the body cannot handle and these are responsible for a very dangerous development — **ketoacidosis**. When the symptoms of diabetes were less readily recognized many patients were not diagnosed until this serious state of affairs had developed, but nowadays there is much more awareness of the condition. Thus ketoacidosis at diagnosis is quite rare unless is has been precipitated by other medical conditions such as pneumonia, gastric disturbances, etc., which tend to speed up its development.

From what has been said before, it is clear that in conditions where there is still some insulin available, the initial symptoms will be less dramatic. Unfortunately this does result in late diagnosis of the condition, so it is very important to be aware and alert for any symptoms, particularly if diabetes has developed in other members of the family. Many diabetics who develop diabetes later in life actually have the diagnosis made when being examined for quite another reason.

What Causes It?'

This is the 'million dollar' question that despite years of intense research and study, can still not be answered with any certainty. It is now understood that people who get diabetes do have a certain susceptibility to its development, which they are born with, i.e. a genetic tendency. However this is less than a quarter of the story, since in many cases diabetes has not previously occurred in a family and in families with diabetes not all individuals are affected. Recent work suggests that it is only if there is an additional 'assault' upon the system that the genetic susceptibility is triggered and the condition develops. The nature of the 'assault' is still far from clear, but infections (particularly viruses), stress, development of obesity (severe overweight) and toxic chemicals have all been implicated. More research, and funds to finance it, are still urgently needed before a definite cause can be identified. The outlook is infinitely more promising than it was, once the cause is known, then prevention through some form of intervention treatment will obviously become a real possibility.

What is certain is that in the condition where insulin production has actually ceased, this can in no way be related to the previous diet. This is very important since many families of young diabetic children are caused severe and quite unnecessary anxiety because of the belief that their child's previous eating habit may have caused the diabetes. The fact that diabetes often occurs following an apparent excess of sweets, i.e. after Christmas or birthday celebrations, is often cited as the reasoning behind such a belief. What is more likely is that the diabetes was developing anyway (due to a genetic susceptibility plus the additional 'assault') and this will have already led to a decrease in the production of insulin in the pancreas. Excess demands (from the consumption of more food) may result in the appearance of symptoms a little sooner because the insulin supply was inadequate for the increased demands, but in no way could it be said that the food had caused the diabetes.

In individuals who get diabetes where insulin injections are not necessary, it is known that the genetic susceptibility is more marked, but again, certain factors may speed up the process. Obesity, while not causing diabetes, is likely to lead to its faster development and thus diagnosis.

Who Gets It and How Is It Treated?

Diabetes is found all over the world, but is much rarer in the poorer, underdeveloped countries, and is very prominent in the affluent Western societies of America, Europe and Scandinavia. In the United Kingdom it is believed that between one and two per cent of the total population have or will develop diabetes. This means that there is upwards of a million individuals in the United Kingdom with diabetes at this very moment.

The condition can present itself at any age but is extremely rare under the age of two, and is very common over the age of fifty-five. If diabetes is diagnosed under the age of twenty-five, almost invariably the person concerned will need daily insulin injections. Over the age of twenty-five treatment is still likely to involve insulin injections. Over the age of forty-five successful treatment without resorting to insulin injections is more likely.

In families containing one or both parents with insulin-dependent diabetes, the likelihood of their children developing insulin-dependent diabetes is greater than if neither parent had diabetes, but the risk is not as pronounced as one would expect. However, in families where there is an insulin-taking diabetic, the likelihood of other members of the family developing diabetes which can be controlled without insulin injections is certainly quite pronounced.

How Is It Treated?
About 30 per cent of all diabetics require a combination of diet and daily insulin injections. The remaining 70 per cent are usually split between control by diet alone (40 per cent) and diet with the addition of hypoglycaemic tablets (30 per cent). Diet is therefore a vital component in the treatment of diabetes. The purpose of the recipes in this book is to illustrate how to put the necessary dietary principles into practice when preparing food for the whole family.

Which Diet?
There is no such thing as a 'diabetic diet'. People need differing quantities of food, therefore all diabetics must receive individual advice on the quantity and timing of their food intake. The information in this book is no substitute for this personal 'tailoring' of advice by a qualified dietitian. In diabetes, dietary changes are needed in order to match the food supply with the available (own or injected) insulin. Large, infrequent meals are hard for the inefficient insulin supply, or the injected insulin, to cope with, therefore it is usually essential to ensure that food intake is spread out across the whole day. Other changes are also necessary, to understand these a brief explanation of digestion is needed.

Digestion
The food we eat in a meal provides a mixture of protein, fat, carbohydrate and water. With this comes a range of vitamins, minerals, trace elements and dietary fibre. Food is chewed, swallowed, and then mixed within the stomach. After the mixing, the food passes into the small intestine where it is broken down into smaller fractions which the body can then use. These 'fractions' are gradually absorbed from the small intestine into the bloodstream and carried to the organs and cells of the body. Here they are used up (metabolized) to provide immediate energy, or stored for future use.

The residue which is left in the intestine is then carried to the large bowel (where much of its water content is removed) and finally excreted. The more fibre (roughage) that is eaten, the greater the quantity of residue and the amount of water retained (because it is bound to the fibre). It is this greater bulk that prevents the development of constipation.

When foods are broken down very quickly, the final fractions (of which glucose is one) arrive in the bloodstream very quickly. If someone has diabetes it is unlikely that their own insulin supply, or that they have injected, can cope with the quantity of glucose that is arriving. As a result the level of glucose in the blood rises rapidly, causing the reappearance of the symptoms of diabetes.

The knowledge of the digestive process has enabled those who look after diabetics to establish basic dietary advice that can be applied to anyone with the condition. This advice is as follows:

1. Do not eat too much food at any one time.
2. Choose meals that are quite slowly digested, thus reducing the excess rise in blood glucose.
3. Plan to eat meals at times that coincide with the availability of plenty of insulin — this is of course relevant when insulin is being taken by injection.

In practice this means that:
a) All diabetics taking insulin, controlled by diet or a combination of diet and tablets are advised to have three or more smallish meals or snacks rather than large meals once or twice a day with large gaps in between.
b) A mixture of food that provides protein, fat and carbohydrate has been shown to take longer to digest. Therefore a 'mixed' meal is better than one that provides mostly carbohydrate or fat or protein. Carbohydrate foods that contain significant amounts of fibre take longer to digest. The fibre seems to act as a sort of packaging which the body has to strip away before it can get on with the breakdown of food into its simpler components. Very sugary foods contain practically no fibre, so they should be avoided as much as possible. If they are eaten, it is best that they are taken with more complex foods which help slow down the release of the glucose into the blood. Of course when a rapid rise in blood glucose is required, for example when injected insulin has not balanced food or activity, causing too low a level of blood glucose, i.e. a hypoglycaemic reaction, such foods are obviously very helpful.

Nowadays stress is laid upon the **right type of carbohydrate, in the right amounts, at the right time.** The amounts and the timing of course must be decided individually. Wherever possible this is planned to fit in with the diabetic's usual lifestyle and eating habits, since diabetes is a life-long condition and a treatment that caters for the disease and not the individual is unlikely to be maintained with any success for any length of time.

Another aspect of the diet plan is the amount of fat that it contains. Fat is a very concentrated source of energy (calories), so it is important to reduce the amount of fat and fatty foods when trying to lose or maintain weight. Due to the value of fibre-rich foods in slowing down the release of glucose, the majority of calories should come from fibre-rich carbohydrate. If the amount of fat is not reduced, then excess total energy (calories) will be eaten, resulting in weight gain.

There is however, an even more persuasive reason for reducing fat intakes — the link between high fat consumption and the development of diseases of the cardiovascular system. It is now recognized that excess fat in the diet is one of the reasons why such conditions are so prevalent in affluent societies. Diabetes itself is a known risk factor in developing such conditions, therefore it is only logical to take steps to decrease other known risk factors as much as possible. A reduction in fat intake, weight loss, if required, and cessation of smoking are all seen as important steps that the diabetic should take as part of their own care. At the moment it is considered reasonable to encourage the use of vegetable fat in preference to fats of animal origin. It is likely that future studies will identify even more closely, the sort of proportions of animal to vegetable fat that should be attained.

All the above considerations will be taken into account when advising an individual on diet. Generally the dietary advice should ensure a correct total energy intake, provided by a balance of approximately 50 per cent carbohydrate, 30-35 per cent fat and 15-20 per cent protein, with at least 25-30 grams of dietary fibre each day. This sort of composition is broadly similar to the 'prudent' diet now advised for the adult population of the United Kingdom.

Which Diet? — A Summary
The diet advised for a diabetic should therefore provide:
— Adequate energy (calories) sufficient to achieve or maintain ideal weight.
— At least half the energy (calories) from carbohydrate foods.
— The majority of carbohydrate coming from fibre-rich sources.
— Reduced amounts of rapidly digested carbohydrates. If these are eaten they should be taken in small amounts as part of a mixed fibre-rich meal.
— A maximum of one third of the total energy (calories) from fat.
— Fats and oils from vegetable sources being taken in preference to animal fat.

Alcohol
Another source of energy (calories) in the diet which has not yet been mentioned, is alcohol. Pure alcohol provides approximately 7 calories per gram, which compares with protein at 4 calories, carbohydrate at 3.75 calories and fat at 9 calories per gram. It is therefore a concentrated source of energy (calories), which has to be taken with great care and considered as part of the diet. A frequent source of confusion arises from the fact that some alcoholic drinks contain carbohydrate and others do not. However, alcohol has a tendency to reduce blood sugar (over a period of 3-6 hours) so the consumption of moderate amounts of carbohydrate within a drink is unlikely to result in a worsening in control. This means that insulin-taking diabetics are not advised to eat less carbohydrate food in an attempt to offset the carbohydrate in an alcoholic drink.

As a general rule, no more than three drinks (half a pint of beer, cider or lager, one pub measure of aperitif, one small glass of sherry, or one glass of wine are considered as one drink) should be taken in any one day. This adds between 200 and 250 extra calories to the diet. This is usually allowed for in the original diet allowance if alcohol is taken on a regular basis. People on weight maintenance or weight reduction diets are usually advised not to have more than one drink for every 1,000 calories of their diet, i.e. one drink on a 1,000 calorie diet, 2 drinks as part of the 2,000 calorie diet and so on.

Some alcoholic drinks contain quite considerable quantities of sugar (15-30 per cent) and these are best avoided, e.g., liqueurs, sweet port, sweet sherries, and sweet vermouths.

If difficulty is encountered in reducing alcohol consumption to the maximum of three drinks a day, it is worth considering making the drinks longer by the addition of mineral water, soda water or sugar-free mixers.

CAUTION: After alcohol consumption driving and other potentially dangerous tasks should not be undertaken because of the increased risk of hypoglycaemia.

Responsibility

No one asks to develop diabetes but once it has developed, the diabetic, with their family and friends, must accept the responsibility for its everyday control. Of course, the various medical, nursing and dietetic advisers should, and do, help, but they can only suggest or guide, they cannot enforce their advice. Frequent checks on overall health and feedback upon the success of treatment from blood and urine testing is essential if optimum treatment and therefore control, is to be achieved.

This chapter has, I hope, emphasized the role of diet and the reasoning behind it, now we can continue and look at how to put that information into practice.

1.

LIVING WITH DIABETES

Obviously someone with diabetes will want to continue to enjoy attractive and interesting meals. The secret of catering for this condition lies in planning and the use of the most suitable ingredients. All the recipes that follow have been developed with the principles of the diet for the diabetic in mind.

Wherever possible, wholegrain, fibre-rich, carbohydrates have been used in preference to their more refined alternatives. The quantity of fat in the recipe has been kept to a minimum and fats of vegetable origin used wherever practicable. The carbohydrate and calorie content and some guidance as to the fibre contribution is given for each recipe. This will ensure that the diabetic can select an appropriate recipe and the quantity of that recipe, to fit in with their own individual diet plan, whether it has been prescribed in terms of carbohydrate, calories, or both. Those without precise allowances to follow are encouraged to use the recipes in the sections to provide a diet containing more fibre and less fat. By careful monitoring of their control and weight, it will become apparent if smaller or larger quantities can be taken in any one day.

Getting Started

Cooking suitable food for someone with diabetes is not (and should not) be an onorous task! All that is necessary is an understanding of the foods to offer, the foods to **use with care,** and foods to actually **encourage.** I hope the recipes in the following sections will act as a stimulus, and in time you will be confident about trying out your own combinations. Much of my 'inspiration' comes from ordinary recipes. It is a relatively easy task to adapt a recipe once you know the type of food you want to substitute in.

At the moment I am concentrating on using more fibre-rich ingredients (especially oats and beans because they contain the best sort of fibre) and cutting back on fat. I look at a recipe for ways in which these small changes can be made — oats in a flan case instead of wheat flour, beans to replace some meat in a casserole and so on. Using this approach there are the occasional disasters, but most of the time you get away with it. When the family want a 'plain meat and two veg' type dinner, that is OK, but remember to keep the fat down by using lean meat, not too much of it — about a 4 oz (100g) cooked portion should suffice. Increase the fibre by serving jacket potatoes, wholewheat pasta or brown rice and plenty of vegetables to accompany a main course.

When you are feeling 'creative' the following tips are worth bearing in mind:

1. Substitute wholemeal flour in sauces and pastry. Use self-raising 100 per cent wholemeal flour with a little extra baking powder for a super sponge.
2. Trim off all visible fat from meat. Allow about 4-6 oz (100-175g) raw weight per person. Usually you will have to reduce the quantity suggested in most recipes.
3. Add cooked or tinned beans or peas to casseroles, soups, etc. Every ounce (25g) of cooked beans adds only 5g of carbohydrate and 20-25 calories, but provides a valuable source of fibre to the meal.
4. Seal meat or vegetables in a minimum of vegetable oil. Often there is no need to use any oil at all if you use a heavy based non-stick pan.
5. Use wholemeal flour to thicken sauces in preference to cornflour or arrowroot.
6. Use a **non-nutritive** (see sweetener notes later) sweetener in fruit, sauces and cheese cakes in place of sugar. Use dried or fresh fruit, or fruit juice in cakes and tea breads for extra fibre and sweetness. If you do need bulk use fruit sugar (fructose) but keep it to a minimum.
7. Use only skimmed milk in cooking. Use skim milk cheeses instead of cream cheese, and reduced fat (15 per cent) cheese in place of full fat cheese wherever possible.
8. Use a reduced fat sunflower spread, or full fat sunflower margarine in place of ordinary butter or margarine. If you need to use shortening use a vegetable version.
9. Always try to use brown rice or wholewheat pasta in place of their more refined alternatives.

The 'Figures'

Someone with diabetes must have their correct amount of carbohydrate and/or calories at each meal. Nevertheless there is always some leeway, so if you are catering for someone with diabetes, there is no need to be over anxious about normal kitchen practices such as slightly thickening gravy (try using wholemeal flour) or tasting a small portion of the final dish. The differences in the final portions are too little to worry about.

However when using the following recipes, or ones that you develop or calculate yourself, care must be taken in measuring the ingredients in order to be certain of the final carbohydrate or calorie contributions. I would heartily recommend buying a accurate set of kitchen scales — I wouldn't be without mine — they are useful for small or large quantities because they read from 1-1000 grams (imperial weighing versions are available) with great accuracy. A clear digital read out is so much easier than a needle on a scale. The facility to return to zero at the press of a button is very useful when measuring out a series of ingredients which are going to end up in the same mixing bowl anyway. I always use a proper set of household measuring spoons for small quantities of wet or dry ingredients because I find the differences when using ordinary cutlery spoons are quite considerable. Last but not least, it is very handy to have a good glass measuring jug which is clearly marked.

With this sort of equipment to hand you can be certain of sufficient accuracy and no chance of destroying all my hard work on the calculations! When devising or adapting your own recipes, use food values information to calculate the content of the final recipe (see worked example below). Do not try to produce a recipe that gives a set amount of carbohydrate — most of the time it won't work. A recipe that looks and tastes good is far better than one that provides the ideal carbohydrate (CHO) or calorie count. Far better a total of 120g CHO and a smaller portion that can be enjoyed, than 100g CHO and a large portion which is inedible.

The carbohydrate and calorie content per portion is determined simply by dividing the total for the recipe by the number of portions made. All the recipes have a suggested number of items or servings, but these are based on average appetites. In many cases less or more can be served depending on circumstances. Just divide the total to obtain the new figures per serving.

An example recipe calculation — 'Profiteroles with Berry Sauce'.

Ingredients	CHO/100g	Cals/100g	Weight used	CHO/Weight (approx.)	Cals/Weight (approx.)
Blackberries	6.0	30	225g	13.5	70
Margarine	—	730	50g	—	365
Wholemeal flour	66.0	320	75g	50.0	240
Eggs × 2	—	150	100g	—	150
Quark cheese	negligible	90	50g	—	45
				63.5	870

$$6 \text{ servings} \therefore 1 \text{ serving} = \frac{63.5}{6} \text{ and } \frac{870}{6}$$

$$= 10.5g \text{ CHO and } 145 \text{ Cals}$$

Notes on Recipe Calculations

I always do my calculations based on the metric weight because most of the nutritional information is available in that form. However if you want to weigh in imperial don't worry, the conversion table I have used is sufficiently accurate to ensure the final 'counts' are not too inaccurate. I always include in the calculations the calorie, carbohydrate and fibre contribution of all the fruit and vegetables.

This is necessary since they are a major contributor in some of the recipes. While vegetables are usually regarded as 'free', this is only in the context of when they are accompaniments to main meals. If I fail to take into account their contribution within the main course, this could significantly underestimate the final calorie and carbohydrate intake. Do not feel that your carbohydrate allowance is being eroded by this, it does ensure that you are having more of your carbohydrate allowance from fibre-rich sources. With diets based on half or more of the total food coming from carbohydrate, you should have more than an adequate allowance anyway. In each recipe I have given total fibre figures (to the nearest 5g) rounded down because some of the available fibre information is rather inaccurate due to differences in methods. Most experts agree that an intake of 25-30 grams of fibre a day is to be recommended. By the side of each recipe title are the initials **'LF'**, i.e. low fibre, **'MF'** i.e. medium fibre, or **'HF'** i.e. high fibre. This refers to the actual contribution per serving to the diet. **'LF'** I have defined as giving less than 5 grams per serving; **'MF'** as giving 5-10 grams per serving, and **'HF'** as providing 10 grams or more per serving. In some of the recipes the total fibre content is quite high but the number of servings are large, this will mean that one or two servings only will result in a small contribution to the fibre intake. Nevertheless wherever possible, recipe ingredients are those that are most rich in fibre, so such servings will provide more fibre than a more refined recipe.

Equipment
I have already mentioned the three pieces of equipment necessary for accurate use of the recipes, but even the most basic kitchen should be able to cope with the recipes in this book. I certainly find my blender and food processor very helpful for speeding up the production of recipes, particularly the processor, in avoiding laborious chopping and slicing. But these are by no means essential. A small pressure cooker is invaluable, not only for the recipes in the pressure cooking section, but also for cooking accompaniments to meals very quickly. The combination of my slow cook and pressure cooker ensures that a meal could be on the table within thirty minutes of arriving home if necessary. This has much to commend it for those cooking with diabetes in mind. Another very good buy is good quality non-stick bakeware which, as well as ensuring minimal amounts of fat are needed to prevent food sticking, also result in more attractive and therefore appealing, finished results. Lastly, in many of the recipes we are avoiding lots of extra fat, and a heavy based set of kitchen ware (I can certainly recommend cast-iron) is a worthwhile investment in which to seal the food.

Sweeteners
Reducing the amount of rapidly absorbed forms of carbohydrate in the diet is an important principle to follow when cooking for a diabetic. Nowadays a

completely sugar-free diet is neither necessary or practical, but it is better that what little sugar is permitted originates from foods pre-sweetened by the food manufacturer and not through use in the home. For this reason the addition of sugar to recipes should be avoided. In many recipes other food ingredients such as fresh and dried fruit and some spices can and do provide adequate sweetness. Where this is insufficient the following guidelines on the use of sweeteners should be followed.

To sweeten only
In many recipes, i.e. jellies, cheese cakes, milk puddings, stewed fruit, custards, etc., there is a need for sweetness, but sugar would not normally be performing any other function. In these circumstances the use of an **'intense'** sweetener is appropriate. Examples of intense sweeteners are Saccharine, Acesulfame Potassium and Aspartame. Such sweeteners provide virtually no calories or carbohydrate and are therefore often referred to as **'non-nutritive'** sweeteners. Such sweeteners can be used by all individuals with diabetes, including those on weight reduction diets. The majority of intense sweeteners are in liquid or tablet form, though there are now available a number of brands of non-nutritive powdered sweeteners (often available in sachet form) which are composed of an intense sweetener, combined with another powder which provides bulk without the same level of intense sweetness. A common bulking combination is saccharine and milk sugar (lactose) or aspartame and milk sugar. This combination results in a powder format which can be sprinkled on to sour fruit, pancakes, cereals, etc. This appeals to many individuals since crushing tablets to perform the same function results in an excessive and cloying sweetness. This is only to be expected since the intense sweeteners are as much as 200 times as sweet as sugar, therefore less than 1/200th of the sweetener can replace the teaspoon of sugar that would normally be sprinkled on a serving of fruit, etc. The combination of milk sugar and an intense sweetener rarely provides more than a maximum of five calories and 1 gram of carbohydrate per sachet, and therefore can be used for most sprinkling purposes. Do not however use this form of sweetener in hot beverages throughout the day. If you did, the carbohydrate and calorie contribution would mount up and will not have been allowed for in the original dietary prescription. Be extremely careful about using other powdered or granulated sweeteners. These usually are a significant source of calories and often carbohydrate (since some brands are a mixture of sugar and saccharine) and thus quite an inappropriate source of calories for the majority of individuals with diabetes. Sweeteners which do provide calories are used to provide bulk and because they are a form of calories, are often referred to as **nutritive** sweeteners. Generally they provide the same number of calories on a weight for weight basis as ordinary sugar, therefore they are only appropriate for a minority of individuals with diabetes and then only under particular

circumstances. This is an area of considerable confusion for those involved in catering for diabetes and details of the suitable sweeteners are given below.

Bulk and sweetening

Sugar's ability to add bulk is an important property and is extensively used in cooking, i.e. in jams and sponges. Also its interaction with other ingredients, particularly fat and flour, can provide specific tastes and textures. Intense sweeteners cannot provide these qualities and if used in large quantities to provide bulk, the final product would be excessively sweet. Similarly they cannot react with fat and flour in the same way as sugar, thus preventing their use in a number of traditional recipes. Clearly there is a need for a sweetener with similar culinary properties to sugar, but which would not result in a rapid rise in blood sugar after consumption. A number of sugar substitutes, e.g., sorbitol, fruit sugar (fructose), isomalt and some hydrogenated glucose syrups, have all been identified as possible sweeteners and are all used in the manufacture of specialized foods.

However, it has become increasingly clear that while such sweeteners appear to have less effect on blood glucose than sugar, they do have an effect if used in more than modest quantities. This is probably due to their calorie contribution and, more importantly, the overall calories contributed by the product in which they are part. In order to minimize the risk of a deterioration in diabetic control, a maximum intake of **a scant ounce (25g)** of one, or a combination of these sweeteners, is recommended in any one day. Readers should bear this in mind when developing recipes themselves, remembering of course to check the contribution from sweeteners in bought specialist products, e.g., preserves, diet pastilles, chewing gum, etc. This contribution must be deducted from the scant ounce (25g) daily allowance.

On a practical level, this limit is not too much of a problem. Most recipes in this book (and the majority of other specialist diabetic recipe books) use minimum quantities of such sweeteners. While quantities per recipe will often exceed the 25 grams, the amount per serving rarely exceeds 5-10 grams. It is unlikely that more than one or two such recipes will be tried in any one day, leaving room for a small quantity of the bought products to be eaten, while still not exceeding the 25 gram maximum.

The limit could all too easily be exceeded if such sweeteners were used as a general sweetener, e.g., on cereals, in hot beverages, etc. Bulk sweeteners are only a maximum of 1½-2 times as sweet (sorbitol alone is less sweet) as sugar, so the quantities used are likely to be similar to that of sugar. As a result the allowance of 25 grams would be used up very quickly, i.e. only 5 level teaspoonfuls. Also, if used in this way, the sweetener is more likely to be digested quicker since it will not have come bound up with the other ingredients, as it would be in baking. This is believed to result in poorer diet control of the diabetes and because of this I strongly recommend that sorbitol, sorbitol/saccharine mixes and fruit sugar (fructose) are **never** used for simple sweetening purposes — they should be used in baking and preserving **only.**

What about the careful use of sugar?
As I already mentioned, some sugar in the diet is inevitable and evidence suggests that in small quantities (particularly as part of a high-fibre diet) it should not be a problem. However the actual amount that can be accommodated is not quite clear, research is currently in progress. It is likely that about 5-8 per cent of the overall calorie intake would not jeopardize diabetic control (people without diabetes currently consume about 20 per cent of their daily calorie intake from sugar). Sugar in small quantities is widely distributed in many processed foods and so features in the diet of most diabetics. Therefore it is easy to exceed the 5-8 per cent of calorie intake if sugar is still being used within the home. Only if minimal amounts of processed foods are eaten, could small amounts of sugar be permitted in baking. At present, however, I am unable to recommend its use to the majority of adults and children with diabetes.

Food Facts
All the foods in the following recipes are widely available. The recipes detail individual ingredients quite clearly, but the reader should read the following notes carefully before turning to the recipe section.

Beans
In the recipes, dried or tinned beans have been specified. If tinned beans are not available, use 5-6 oz (150-175g) of dried beans (soaked and cooked in the normal way) to replace one large (15½ oz/425g) tin of beans in the recipe. There is no need to avoid tinned beans that mention sugar in the ingredient list since the quantity used is always small and the majority is lost during the rinsing and draining procedure. Where dry beans have been specified remember to soak overnight or bring to the boil and cover for a minimum of two hours. The beans must then be cooked as directed. It is vital that all dried beans are brought to the boil and held at boiling point for at least ten minutes before reducing the heat and cooking in either a covered pan or pressure cooker. I recommend discarding any cooking liquor used in boiling the beans and adding a tablespoonful of cider or wine vinegar, or spices such as ginger or garlic (recipe *permitting*) during cooking, as this appears to reduce the problem of wind (flatulence) in most susceptible people.

Dairy products
Always use skimmed-milk in cooking. When cooking for children under the age of ten who are not drinking any whole milk in their diet, a better choice might be semi-skimmed milk for cooking purposes. This will add the same amount of carbohydrate, but the calories of the final recipe will be slightly more since

a pint of skimmed-milk provides a maximum of 200 calories compared to 250-300 calories for a pint of semi-skimmed milk. Fresh, long-life or sterilized skimmed milk can be used (as available) in all recipes. Cream has been avoided wherever possible as it is a major source of fat, but if cream is going to be served to accompany a recipe, select a single cream wherever possible.

Fats and oils
In the recipes using oil, sunflower oil has been specified since it gives a better flavour and is one of the most widely available polyunsaturated oils. Other polyunsaturated oils can be selected providing their taste is acceptable to the family.

Other recipes use a sunflower margarine as a means of increasing the amount of polyunsaturated fat in the diet and providing essential fatty acids. Since there is ample evidence to suggest that a reduced fat diet can help reduce the risk of coronary heart disease, in all recipes added fat has been kept to a minimum. Where successful, I have specified a reduced-fat sunflower spread which offers the benefit of a polyunsaturated fat, but with less than half the fat of a normal vegetable margarine or butter. Where a shortening agent was necessary a vegetable shortening has been specified, this is preferable to lard which is animal based.

Fish
Frozen fish can be substituted in place of fresh fish in any recipe. Where tinned fish has been specified ensure that it is bought in brine or alternatively in tomato sauce, removing the tomato sauce if it is not appropriate to the recipe.

Eggs
All the recipes have been tested with the size of egg specified. If smaller eggs are used, usually a little extra liquid in the recipe will be necessary. Free range or standard eggs can be used as available or preferred.

Flour
Always use a flour labelled as 'wholemeal' or 'wholewheat'. Unless specified as self-raising in the recipe, this is the type of flour to use. If a 100 per cent self-raising wholemeal flour has been specified but is not available, then you may use a standard wholemeal/wholewheat flour (try to avoid ones labelled as bread flour) with extra baking powder. This will give a reasonable rise, but the final product is unlikely to have such a light texture.

Fruit
Frozen fruit can be substituted for fresh fruit in the recipes providing it is not sugar or syrup packed. If tinned fruit in natural juice has been specified in a recipe, fresh or frozen fruit can be substituted instead. However you will usually need approximately one and a half times the tin weight to maintain the calculations based on the fruit in natural juice. The fresh or frozen fruit should be cooked in a little water until slightly softened before proceeding with the normal recipe instructions.

Herbs

In all the recipes quantities of herbs are based on the dried versions unless specifically described as fresh. If fresh herbs are available these can add a more delicate flavour, though usually a little more is necessary to achieve the same taste.

Meat

In all the recipes assume the weight given is based on the meat as purchased including any bone or any waste that will be trimmed away before preparation. If a weight is referring to meat only it will be described as a quantity of 'boned meat'. In all the recipes, in order to reduce total fat intake, buy as lean a cut as you can and trim off all visible fat before following the recipe instructions. When buying mince, try to buy the best quality or alternatively a lean cut which you or your butcher can mince.

Nuts

Unless specified, all weights of nuts refer to the kernel only and not the weight before shelling. There is no need to buy ground nuts if you have a liquidizer or processor as these will easily cope with grinding the nuts. Remember to lightly roast the nuts in a hot oven and remove the skin before grinding.

Oats

There is no need to buy oatmeal as such, as ordinary rolled (porridge) oats can be made into oatmeal using a blender or processor. This saves on storage space and works out cheaper.

Seasoning

In all the recipes freshly ground black pepper has been specified as this gives a better flavour. However ground black or white pepper can be used if preferred. Sea salt has been specified as this imparts more flavour than ordinary table salt and enables the quantities to be substantially reduced. If you wish to cut back further on salt in the diet the quantities can be reduced further or omitted in most recipes.

Spices

The quantities of spice are based on reasonable, but not excessively strong flavouring of the final recipe. If you like a more pronounced taste extra spice can be used without effecting the final recipe calculations or the appearance of the recipe. It is always best to buy spices in small quantities and store them away from the light as this maintains their flavour and colouring.

Sweeteners

The majority of recipes use non-nutritive liquid or powder sweeteners as these add sweetness without extra calories or carbohydrate. Where bulk has been necessary, minimal amounts of fruit sugar have been used. **See sweetener notes for more detail.**

2.

COOKER-TOP RECIPES

Green Pea Soup with Herb Dumplings (HF)

(Serves 4)

Total Fibre = 50g
Total Calories = 600
Total Carbohydrate = 80g
Each serving contains 20g and 150 calories

The Soup:

Imperial (Metric)
2 pints (1.1l) chicken stock
1 lb (450g) frozen green peas
1 medium onion, finely chopped
Freshly ground pepper
Pinch of sea salt
1 teaspoon cayenne pepper

American
5 cups chicken stock
1 pound frozen green peas
1 medium onion, finely chopped
Freshly ground pepper
Pinch of sea salt
1 teaspoon cayenne pepper

The Dumplings:

Imperial (Metric)
3 oz (75g) wholemeal flour
1 tablespoon wheat bran
2 teaspoons baking powder
½ teaspoon thyme
Pinch of sea salt
Freshly ground black pepper
2 teaspoons sunflower oil
Warm water to mix

American
¾ cup wholewheat flour
1 tablespoon wheat bran
2 teaspoons baking powder
½ teaspoon thyme
Pinch of sea salt
Freshly ground black pepper
2 teaspoons sunflower oil
Warm water to mix

1. Place all the soup ingredients in a large pan. Bring to the boil, cover, reduce heat and simmer.

2. Meanwhile, combine all the dry ingredients for the dumplings together. Add the oil and sufficient warm water to mix to a soft dough. Quickly form into 12 small balls.

3. Drop into the simmering soup. Replace the cover and continue cooking until the dumplings are cooked through (about 20-30 minutes).

4. Serve immediately. Alternatively, carefully remove the dumplings, place in a serving dish and keep warm in the oven. Process or liquidize the soup. Reheat gently adding the dumplings just before serving.

Note: The puréed soup freezes well but the dumplings are better freshly prepared. If frozen soup is available, then dumplings can be freshly made using chicken or vegetable stock for the cooking liquid.

Tomato and Rice Soup (LF)
'Use dark red tomatoes for the best results'

(Serves 6)

Total Fibre = 10g
Total Calories = 450
Total Carbohydrate = 90g
Each serving contains 15g CHO and 75 calories

Imperial (Metric)	American
1 large onion, finely chopped	1 large onion, finely chopped
1 teaspoon sunflower oil	1 teaspoon sunflower oil
2 lbs (900g) red tomatoes, skinned	2 pounds red tomatoes
3 oz (75g) brown rice	3 ounces brown rice
1½ pints (850ml) chicken or vegetable stock	3¾ cups chicken or vegetable stock
½ pint (275ml) tomato juice	1⅓ cups tomato juice
Sea salt	Sea salt
Freshly ground black pepper	Freshly ground black pepper

1. Sweat the onions in the oil in a covered pan until softened.

2. Roughly chop or process the tomatoes. Add the tomatoes, rice, stock and tomato juice to the onions. Stir and season well.

3. Bring to the boil — reduce heat and simmer for approximately 1 hour or until rice is tender. Serve. *Do not freeze.*

Mushroom Soup (LF)
'with a zest'

(Serves 4)

Total Fibre = 10g
Total Calories = 220
Total Carbohydrate = negligible
Each serving contains negligible CHO and 55 calories

Imperial (Metric)	**American**
1 tablespoon sunflower oil	1 tablespoon sunflower oil
1 lb (450g) cup mushrooms, finely sliced	1 pound cup mushrooms, finely sliced
2 medium onions, finely chopped	2 medium onions, finely chopped
1½ pints (850ml) chicken stock	3¾ cups chicken stock
Juice of a large lemon	Juice of a large lemon
Freshly ground black pepper	Freshly ground black pepper
Sea salt	Sea salt
4 thin slices of lemon	4 thin slices of lemon

1. Heat the oil in a heavy pan. Add the mushrooms and onions. Cover, continue cooking gently until softened.

2. Add the stock and lemon juice and season well. Cover the pan again and simmer for 30-45 minutes.

3. Liquidize or process until smooth. *Freeze at this point if required.* Return to pan and heat thoroughly, adjusting seasoning as necessary.

4. Serve garnished with lemon slices.

Cauliflower Cheese (MF)
Illustrated opposite page 32.
(Serves 2)

Total Fibre = 15g
Total Calories = 480
Total Carbohydrate = 40g
Each serving contains 20g CHO and 240 calories

Imperial (Metric)	**American**
1 small (1 lb/450g) cauliflower, trimmed	1 small (1 pound) cauliflower, trimmed
1 medium green or red pepper, diced	1 medium green or red pepper, diced
1 medium onion, finely chopped	1 medium onion, finely chopped
½ pint (275ml) skimmed milk	1⅓ cups skimmed milk
2 tablespoons wholemeal flour	2 tablespoons wholewheat flour
1 tablespoon sunflower margarine	1 tablespoon sunflower margarine
A good pinch of thyme and mixed herbs	A good pinch of thyme and mixed herbs
Freshly ground black pepper	Freshly ground black pepper
Pinch of sea salt	Pinch of sea salt
4 oz (100g) button mushrooms, sliced	4 ounces button mushrooms, sliced
1 oz (25g) reduced fat (15%) hard cheese, grated	1 ounce reduced fat (15%) hard cheese, grated

1. Break the cauliflower into small pieces. Cook for just under 10 minutes in boiling salted water, remove using draining spoon before quite cooked. Drain well and place in a warmed ovenproof dish.

2. Blanch the pepper and onion in the cauliflower water. Drain.

3. Meanwhile combine the milk, flour, margarine, herbs and seasoning. Cook over a gentle heat until thickened, stirring continuously.

4. Add the blanched pepper, onion and the sliced mushrooms. Continue cooking for a minute or two.

5. Pour the sauce over the cauliflower, then sprinkle over the cheese. Brown in a hot oven or under the grill until cheese is melted and the whole dish is completely heated through. *Do not freeze.*

6. Serve with a green vegetable and wholemeal bread or wholewheat pasta or jacket potatoes.

Lentils with Spiced Rice (MF)

(Serves 3)

Total Fibre = 15g
Total Calories = 780
Total Carbohydrate = 150g
Each serving contains 50g CHO and 260 calories

Imperial (Metric)
3 oz (75g) whole green lentils, rinsed
1 medium onion, chopped
5 oz (150g) brown rice
2 teaspoons hot curry powder
1 teaspoon cardamom
1 small green or red pepper, diced
Garnish — cooked frozen peas,
   chopped parsley and tomato slices

American
3 ounces whole green lentils, rinsed
1 medium onion, chopped
5 ounces brown rice
2 teaspoons hot curry powder
1 teaspoon cardamom
1 small green or red pepper, diced
Garnish — cooked frozen peas,
   chopped parsley and tomato slices

1. Cook the lentils in water until tender — about 40 minutes. After 30 minutes add the chopped onion.

2. Meanwhile place the rice in a large pan half full of boiling salted water. Add the curry and cardamom. Cover, reduce heat and leave to cook until nearly all the water is absorbed.

3. Add the diced pepper, then cover the pan again and continue cooking until the rice is tender (but not mushy). Note — if the water is not all absorbed remove cover, increase heat and cook until all the excess water is removed, taking care not to let the rice 'catch' on the base.

4. Drain the lentils very well. Stir into the rice and serve immediately garnished with freshly cooked frozen peas, parsley and tomatoes. A little fruit pickle is an ideal slightly sweet accompaniment or alternatively add a tablespoon of sultanas to the cooking rice 5 minutes before serving.

5. *Do not freeze.* But the rice can be served cold.

Opposite: Cauliflower Cheese ready for its low-fat topping (page 31).

Saucy Tuna (LF)

(Serves 2)

Total Fibre = negligible
Total Calories = 500
Total Carbohydrate = 20g
Each serving contains 10g CHO and 250 calories

Imperial (Metric)
1 small onion, finely chopped
1 oz (25g) sunflower margarine
2 tablespoons wholemeal flour
⅓ pint (200ml) skimmed milk
¼ teaspoon mixed herbs
Freshly ground black pepper
1×7oz (200g) tin tuna in brine,
   drained and flaked

American
1 small onion, finely chopped
2½ tablespoons sunflower margarine
2 tablespoons wholewheat flour
¾ cup skimmed milk
¼ teaspoon mixed herbs
Freshly ground black pepper
1×7 ounce can tuna in brine,
   drained and flaked

1. Soften the onion in the margarine.

2. Stir in the flour and continue cooking for a minute or two.

3. Whisk in the milk, herbs and pepper and continue cooking over a low heat for 5 minutes.

4. Stir in the tuna. Simmer for a further 5 minutes.

5. Serve with wholewheat pasta shells or creamed potatoes, whole green beans and mixed vegetables and garnished with lemon slices or paprika. *Do not freeze.*

Opposite: Pretty as a picture, Profiteroles with Berry Sauce (page 50).

Oat-Topped Cod (LF)

(Serves 2)

Total Fibre = 5g
Total Calories = 750
Total Carbohydrate = 70g
Each serving contains 35g CHO and 375 calories

Imperial (Metric)
12 oz (350g) cod fillet, skinned
¼ pint (150ml) skimmed milk
1 teaspoon dried tarragon
Freshly ground black pepper
1 large onion, finely chopped
1 tablespoon sunflower margarine
3 oz (75g) porridge oats
Pinch of sea salt

American
12 ounce cod fillet, skinned
⅔ cup skimmed milk
1 teaspoon dried tarragon
Freshly ground black pepper
1 large onion, finely chopped
1 tablespoon sunflower margarine
¾ cup rolled oats
Pinch of sea salt

1. Poach the fish in the milk with the tarragon in a covered pan.

2. Gently sauté the onion in the margarine.

3. Remove the fish from the heat.

4. Drain the milk liquor off and pour onto the onion mixture.

5. Stir in the oats and continue cooking gently until the sauce thickens. When cooked spread over the fish.

6. Brown under a grill or in a hot oven. Serve garnished with whole green beans or tomato slices. *Do not freeze.*

Wholewheat Pasta with Chicken (MF)

(Serves 4)

Total Fibre = 20g
Total Calories = 1200
Total Carbohydrate = 120g
Each serving contains 30g CHO and 300 calories

Imperial (Metric)	American
1 teaspoon sunflower oil	1 teaspoon sunflower oil
1 lb (450g) boned chicken, cubed	1 pound boned chicken, cubed
1 teaspoon fennel seeds	1 teaspoon fennel seeds
1 small onion, diced	1 small onion, diced
Sea salt	Sea salt
Freshly ground black pepper	Freshly ground black pepper
½ teaspoon paprika	½ teaspoon paprika
2 tablespoons wholemeal flour	2 tablespoons wholewheat flour
⅓ pint (200ml) skimmed milk	¾ cup skimmed milk
5 oz (150g) wholewheat pasta shells	5 ounces wholewheat pasta shells

1. Heat the oil in a heavy based pan.

2. Mix the chicken, fennel seeds, onion and seasoning together.

3. Brown in the pan, reduce the heat and continue cooking for 2-3 minutes.

4. Increase the heat, stir in the flour, continue cooking for a minute, then add the milk. Stir well until thickening. Reduce the heat and cover again. Simmer for 10-15 minutes.

5. While the sauce is simmering, cook the wholewheat pasta shells in salted boiling water. When cooked drain well.

6. To serve, either combine the drained pasta and sauce or serve the pasta and the sauce separately. Garnish with whole green beans or cooked frozen peas. *Do not freeze.*

Creamy Beef and Courgette (HF)

(Serves 4)

Total Fibre = 40g
Total Calories = 1040
Total Carbohydrate = 100g
Each serving contains 25g CHO and 260 calories

Imperial (Metric)
8 oz (225g) minced steak
1 lb (450g) courgettes, sliced
1 large onion, sliced
1 large red pepper, chopped
1×15 oz (425g) tin borlotti beans, drained
1×14 oz (400g) tin chopped tomatoes
3 oz (75g) frozen green peas
1 packet 6 oz (175g) firm tofu
1×5.3 oz (150g) pot low-fat natural yogurt
1 teaspoon sea salt
Freshly ground black pepper

American
8 ounces minced steak
1 pound zucchini, sliced
1 large onion, sliced
1 large red pepper, chopped
1×15 ounce can pinto beans, drained
1×14 ounce can chopped tomatoes
½ cup frozen green peas
1 packet 6 ounce firm tofu
⅔ cup low fat plain yogurt
1 teaspoon sea salt
Freshly ground black pepper

1. Gently cook the minced steak in a large heavy bottomed pan until browned. Drain off any fat.

2. Add the courgettes, onion and pepper. Mix over the heat for 5-10 minutes.

3. Add the drained beans, tomatoes and peas. Cover and cook for 10 minutes.

4. Meanwhile blend the tofu and yogurt with the seasoning.

5. Remove the cover from meat and vegetables. Gently stir in the tofu and yogurt mixture — continue cooking over a gentle heat until heated through.

6. Serve immediately with whole green beans and brown rice or wholemeal pittas. *Do not freeze.*

Pancakes (LF)

(Makes 6)

Total Fibre = 5g
Total Calories = 420
Total Carbohydrate = 60g
Each serving contains 10g CHO and 70 calories

Imperial (Metric)	**American**
3 oz (75g) wholemeal flour	¾ cup wholewheat flour
1 size 3 egg, beaten	1 size 3 egg, beaten
⅓ pint (200ml) skimmed milk	¾ cup skimmed milk
¼ pint (150ml) cold water	⅔ cup cold water
Pinch of sea salt	Pinch of sea salt
Sunflower oil	Sunflower oil

1. Whisk all the ingredients together except the oil. Cover and leave to stand for an hour (if possible).

2. Heat a 6-7 inch (15-17cm) non-stick frying pan or griddle. Lightly oil.

3. Drop a few tablespoonsful of the mixture into the hot pan. Spread thinly by turning the pan.

4. Cook over the medium heat then flip over using a spatula. Cook until brown — usually 1-2 minutes each side.

5. Turn onto a plate and keep warm over a pan of water or in a cool oven.

6. Repeat the process making 6 pancakes in all. Use for a savoury or sweet filling.

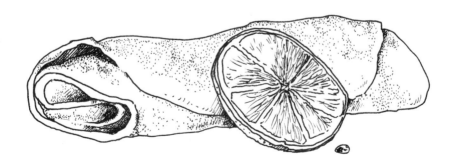

Mexican Beef (LF)

Fills 6 pancakes

Total Fibre = 10g
Total Calories = 330
Total Carbohydrate = 20g
Each serving contains negligible CHO and 55 calories

Imperial (Metric)	**American**
8 oz (225g) carrots, grated	8 ounces carrots, grated
1 medium onion, chopped	1 medium onion, chopped
1 teaspoon sunflower oil	1 teaspoon sunflower oil
1 medium red pepper, diced	1 medium red pepper, diced
3 oz (75g) corned beef	3 ounces corned beef
3 oz (75g) frozen green peas	½ cup frozen green peas
¼ teaspoon hot chilli sauce	¼ teaspoon hot chilli sauce
¼ teaspoon hot chilli powder	¼ teaspoon hot chilli powder
¼ teaspoon soya sauce	¼ teaspoon soy sauce
¼ teaspoon ground ginger	¼ teaspoon ground ginger
Freshly ground black pepper	Freshly ground black pepper

1. Soften the carrot and onion in the oil in a heavy-based pan.

2. Add the pepper, corned beef, peas, spices and soya sauce.

3. Cover and cook gently for 10-15 minutes.

4. Use to fill the pancakes (see page 37).

Wholewheat Dropscones (LF)

(Makes 15 dropscones)

Total Fibre = 30g
Total Calories = 750
Total Carbohydrate = 150g
Each dropscone contains 10g CHO and 50 calories

Imperial (Metric)	**American**
5 oz (150g) self-raising wholemeal flour	1¼ cups self-raising wholewheat flour
⅓ pint (200ml) skimmed milk	¾ cup skimmed milk
1 size 3 egg	1 size 3 egg
3 oz (75g) dried apricots, finely chopped	½ cup finely chopped dried apricots

1. Whisk the flour, milk and egg together.

2. Add the dried apricots. Cover and leave to stand overnight, then beat again before using.

3. Heat a lightly oiled, heavy-based frying pan (or a griddle).

4. Drop spoonfuls of the mixture into the hot pan.

5. Cook for 2-3 minutes. Turn and continue until golden brown and cooked right through, turning again if necessary. Flatten a little if thick.

6. Continue cooking (re-oiling pan if necessary) until all the mixture is used — making 15 dropscones in all. *(Freeze at this point if desired).*

7. Serve on their own or lightly spread with a low-fat spread and sugar-free fruit preserves.

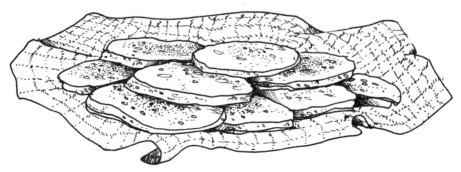

3.

USING YOUR OVEN

Sunday Chicken (LF)

(Serves 2)

Total Fibre = 5g
Total Calories = 750
Total Carbohydrate = 20g
Each serving contains 10g CHO and 375 calories

Imperial (Metric)
1 clove garlic
Sea salt
2 skinned chicken portions on the
   bone (20 oz/550g)
1 measure (⅓ gill/50ml) Rosso
   vermouth
4 oz (100g) button mushrooms
2 rashers lean smoked bacon
   (2 oz/50g), trimmed
1 medium onion, chopped
1 small green pepper, diced
1 tablespoon tomato purée
¼ pint (150ml) chicken stock
1×14 oz (400g) tin chopped
   tomatoes
2 leaves fresh basil

American
1 clove garlic
Sea salt
2 skinned chicken portions on the
   bone (20 ounces)
⅓ gill Rosso vermouth
4 ounces button mushrooms
2 rashers (2 ounces) lean smoked
   bacon, trimmed
1 medium onion, chopped
1 small green pepper, diced
1 tablespoon tomato paste
⅔ cup chicken stock
1×14 ounce can chopped tomatoes
2 leaves fresh basil

1. Crush the garlic with the sea salt, rub over the skinned chicken.

2. Put the chicken and garlic in an ovenproof dish. Cover and brown in a hot oven for 10-15 minutes. Pour over the vermouth and add the mushrooms.

3. Meanwhile cook the bacon, onion and pepper in a non-stick heavy-based pan until the bacon is browned, drain off any fat.

4. Add the tomato purée (paste), chicken stock and the chopped tomatoes and basil.

5. Pour over the chicken. Cover and continue cooking in a hot oven 350°F/190°C (Gas Mark 5) until the chicken is tender.

6. Serve with boiled brown rice or wholewheat pitta breads and spring cabbage.

Corn Sausage Meat Stuffing (LF)

(Serves 6 — good helpings)

Total Fibre = 10g
Total Calories = 1080
Total Carbohydrate = 60g
Each serving contains 10g CHO and 180 calories

Imperial (Metric)	American
½ lb (225g) pork sausage meat	½ pound pork sausage meat
3 oz (75g) fresh wholemeal or granary breadcrumbs	1½ cups fresh wholewheat breadcrumbs
1 tablespoon tomato purée	1 tablespoon tomato paste
1 teaspoon mixed herbs	1 teaspoon mixed herbs
Freshly ground black pepper	Freshly ground black pepper
1 egg, beaten	1 egg, beaten
3 oz (75g) tinned sweetcorn	½ cup canned sweetcorn

1. Mix the sausage meat, breadcrumbs, tomato purée (paste), herbs and pepper together. Add the egg and mix well.

2. Stir in the sweetcorn.

3. Press into a non-stick baking dish (approx 6-inch diameter). Smooth surface and bake in a pre-heated oven at 375°F/190°C (Gas Mark 5) until brown — about 30-40 minutes. Remove any surface fat with a little kitchen roll. *Freeze at this point if desired.*

4. Cut into 6 — serve while still hot with poultry.

Pork and Port (LF)

(Serves 2)

Total Fibre = negligible
Total Calories = 380
Total Carbohydrate = negligible
Each serving contains negligible CHO and 190 calories

Imperial (Metric)
2 small pork steaks (8 oz/225g) in
    total *or* 2 small pork loin chops
Pinch of chilli
Freshly ground black pepper
2 teaspoons Dijon mustard
2 tablespoons water
1 small green pepper
1 small onion, chopped
2 oz (50g) button mushrooms, sliced
2 tablespoons Dry Port

American
2 small pork steaks *or* 2 small pork
    loin chops
Pinch of chili
Freshly ground black pepper
2 teaspoons Dijon mustard
2 tablespoons water
1 small green pepper
1 small onion, chopped
2 ounces button mushrooms, sliced
2 tablespoons Dry Port

1. Trim off all visible fat from the pork. Place in an oven-proof dish. Mix the spices, mustard and water together. Pour over the steaks/chops.

2. Cut the pepper into strips. Blanch with the onions until slightly softened. Drain, sprinkle over the meat.

3. Add the mushrooms. Pour over the Port. Cover.

4. Bake at 375°F/190°C (Gas Mark 5) for 30-45 minutes or until meat is tender.

5. Remove cover, continue cooking until the meat is browned. *This freezes well.*

6. Serve with brown rice or jacket potatoes.

Bramley Stuffing (LF)

'A refreshing accompaniment to pork or poultry'

(Serves 6)

Total Fibre = 5g
Total Calories = 960
Total Carbohydrate = 60g
Each serving contains 10g CHO and 160 calories

Imperial (Metric)

1 large cooking apple, finely
   chopped or grated
8 oz (225g) pork sausage meat
1 oz (25g) bulghar (cracked wheat)
1 teaspoon sage
1 teaspoon savory
Freshly ground black pepper

American

1 large cooking apple, finely
   chopped or grated
8 ounces pork sausage meat
1 ounce bulghar (cracked wheat)
1 teaspoon sage
1 teaspoon savory
Freshly ground black pepper

1. Mix (or process) all the ingredients together.

2. Press into a non-stick ovenproof dish (approx 6-inch diameter).

3. Bake in a preheated oven at 375°F/190°C (Gas Mark 5) for 20-30 minutes
   until brown and slightly dry. *Freeze at this point if desired.*

4. Cut into 6 and serve hot or cold with pork or poultry.

Liver and Vegetable Casserole (MF)

(Serves 4)

Total Fibre = 20g
Total Calories = 960
Total Carbohydrate = 80g
Each serving contains 20g CHO and 240 calories

Imperial (Metric)
½ pint (275ml) beef stock
12 oz (350g) pigs liver, cubed
1 medium onion, sliced
1 teaspoon paprika
1 lb (450g) courgettes, sliced
1×15½ oz (440g) tin butter beans,
  drained
1×14 oz (400g) tin chopped
  tomatoes
1 tablespoon tomato purée
1 teaspoon basil
Freshly ground black pepper
Pinch of sea salt

American
1⅓ cups beef stock
12 ounces pigs liver, cubed
1 medium onion, sliced
1 teaspoon paprika
1 pound zucchini, sliced
1×15½ ounce can lima beans,
  drained
1×14 ounce can chopped tomatoes
1 tablespoon tomato paste
1 teaspoon basil
Freshly ground black pepper
Pinch of sea salt

1. Simmer the stock, liver, onion and paprika in a covered pan for 10-15 minutes.

2. Add the courgettes (zucchini), beans, tomato.

3. Stir in the tomato purée (paste), add the basil and the seasoning. Cover and cook in a pre-heated oven at 400°F/200°C (Gas Mark 6) for 45 minutes. *Freeze at this point if desired.*

4. Serve with jacket potatoes and cauliflower.

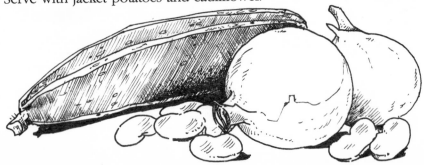

Yorkshire Puddings (LF)

(Makes 12)

Total Fibre = 5g
Total Calories = 420
Total Carbohydrate = 60g
Each Yorkshire contains 5g CHO and 35 calories

Imperial (Metric)
3 oz (75g) wholemeal flour
1 size 3 egg, beaten
⅓ pint (200ml) skimmed milk
Pinch of sea salt

American
¾ cup wholewheat flour
1 size 3 egg, beaten
¾ cup skimmed milk
Pinch of sea salt

1. Place the flour in the mixing bowl.

2. Add the egg, milk and salt and whisk well.

3. Cover and leave to stand for at least half an hour.

4. Whisk again.

5. Lightly oil a warmed 12 bun deep patty tin.

6. Spoon the mixture into the 12 moulds.

7. Place in the pre-heated oven and bake at 425°F/220°C (Gas Mark 7) for about 15 minutes or until the Yorkshires are risen and set. *Do not freeze.*

Yogurt Bread (LF)

(Cuts into 20 good slices)

Total Fibre = 50g
Total Calories = 2200
Total Carbohydrate = 400g
Each slice contains 20g CHO and 110 calories

Imperial (Metric)	American
1 pint (550ml) low-fat natural yogurt	2½ cups low-fat plain yogurt
3 oz (75g) raisins	½ cup raisins
1 teaspoon sunflower oil	1 teaspoon sunflower oil
1 lb (450g) wholemeal flour	4 cups wholewheat flour
1 teaspoon bicarbonate of soda	1 teaspoon baking soda
2 teaspoons cinnamon	2 teaspoons cinnamon
3 tablespoons sesame seeds	3 tablespoons sesame seeds
1 size 3 egg, beaten	1 size 3 egg, beaten

1. Mix the yogurt, raisins and oil together.

2. Place the flour, soda, cinnamon and 2 tablespoons of the sesame seeds in the mixing bowl.

3. Lightly oil a 2 pound (900g) loaf tin, sprinkle top and sides with the remaining sesame seeds.

4. Pour the yogurt mixture into the bowl. Beat well until the mixture forms a soft dough. Add the beaten egg and continue mixing until the mixture is a stiff dropping consistency.

5. Transfer the dough to the loaf tin, smooth top.

6. Bake at 375°F/190°C (Gas Mark 5) for approximately 1 hour 15 minutes, until brown and risen — the base will sound hollow when cooked through.

7. Turn out onto a cooling rack. When cold, cut into slices. *This freezes well.*

Crunchy Blackcurrants (HF)

(Serves 4)

Total Fibre = 40g
Total Calories = 800
Total Carbohydrate = 80g
Each serving contains 20g CHO and 200 calories

Imperial (Metric)
12 oz (350g) fresh or frozen
  blackcurrants, washed
A little non-nutritive sweetener
  (optional)
3 oz (75g) self-raising wholemeal
  flour
1 oz (25g) desiccated coconut
1 tablespoon fruit sugar (fructose)
1 oz (25g) sunflower margarine
1 egg yolk, beaten
½ teaspoon cinnamon

American
3 cups blackcurrants, washed
A little non-nutritive sweetener
  (optional)
¾ cup self-raising wholewheat flour
⅓ cup desiccated coconut
1 tablespoon fruit sugar (fructose)
2½ tablespoons sunflower margarine
1 egg yolk, beaten
½ teaspoon cinnamon

1. Place the fruit in a small (6-7-inch diameter) ovenproof dish, sweeten to taste.

2. Mix the remaining ingredients together to form a 'breadcrumb texture'.

3. Sprinkle evenly over the fruit.

4. Bake in a pre-heated oven 325°F/160°C (Gas Mark 3) for about 30 minutes or until topping is golden and crunchy.

5. Divide into 4 servings and serve with a little natural yogurt, custard or evaporated milk as preferred.

Coconut Cutting Cake (LF)

(Makes 20 slices)

Total Fibre = 40g
Total Calories = 2400
Total Carbohydrate = 200g
Each serving contains 10g CHO and 120 calories

Imperial (Metric)
8 oz (225g) wholemeal self-raising
   flour
1 teaspoon baking powder
3 oz (75g) desiccated coconut
3 oz (75g) fructose (fruit sugar)
⅛ pint (75ml) sunflower oil
¼ pint (150ml) skimmed milk
2 size 3 eggs, beaten
Juice and rind of a large lemon

American
2 cups wholewheat self-raising flour
1 teaspoon baked powder
1 cup desiccated coconut
3 ounces fruit sugar (fructose)
¼ cup sunflower oil
⅔ cup skimmed milk
2 size 3 eggs, beaten
Juice and rind of a large lemon

1. Place the flour, baking powder, coconut and fructose in the mixing bowl.

2. Add the oil, milk, egg and lemon. Beat well or use a mixer or processor to mix the mixture.

3. Turn into a non-stick or lightly oiled 2 pound (900g) loaf tin.

4. Bake in the middle of the oven at 350°F/180°C (Gas Mark 4) until brown and risen. Approximately 1 hour. Leave to cool before turning out. Cuts into 20 slices.

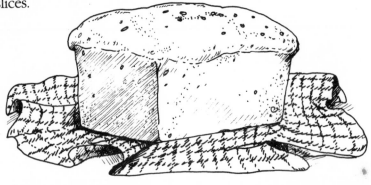

Opposite: Rich and full of flavour, Vichy Bean Soup (page 53).

Date and Apple Cake (LF)

(Makes 16 slices)

Total Fibre = 55g
Total Calories = 2080
Total Carbohydrate = 320g
Each slice contains 20g CHO and 130 calories

Imperial (Metric)
½ pint (275ml) boiling weak tea
4 oz (100g) stoned dates, finely
   chopped
1 oz (25g) desiccated coconut
1 large cooking apple, finely
   chopped
12 oz (350g) self-raising wholemeal
   flour
3 tablespoons sunflower oil
2 teaspoons ground ginger
1 teaspoon baking powder

American
1⅓ cups boiling weak tea
4 ounces stoned dates, finely
   chopped
⅓ cup desiccated coconut
⅓ cup cooking apple, finely
   chopped
3 cups wholewheat self-raising flour
3 tablespoons sunflower oil
2 teaspoons ground ginger
1 teaspoon baking powder

1. Pour the tea over the dates. Leave to stand for at least 1 hour.

2. Place the coconut, apple, flour, oil and ginger in a mixing bowl.

3. Pour on the date mixture. Mix well, use a food mixer if available. Add the baking powder. Mix again.

4. Turn into a non-stick or lightly oiled 9-inch (23cm)/2 pound (900g) loaf tin. Smooth the top.

5. Bake at 375°F/190°C (Gas Mark 5) for approximately 1¼-1½ hours, until brown and risen. Cover with greaseproof or foil after 1 hour if browning before thoroughly cooked. Turn out when cool. *This freezes well.*

Opposite: Full of health, Cabbage Packages (page 67).

Profiteroles with Berry Sauce (LF)
Illustrated opposite page 33.
(Serves 6)

Total Fibre = 25g
Total Calories = 980 (with cream)
　　　　or = 870 (with low-fat soft cheese)
Total Carbohydrate = 60g
Each serving contains 10g CHO and 165 (or 145) calories

Sauce:

Imperial (Metric)	**American**
8 oz (225g) blackberries/currants	2 cups blackberries/currants
1-2 tablespoons water	1-2 tablespoons water
Liquid or non-nutritive powder sweetener	Liquid or non-nutritive sweetener

Choux Pastry:

Imperial (Metric)	**American**
¼ pint (150ml) water	⅔ cup water
2 oz (50g) sunflower margarine	¼ cup sunflower margarine
3 oz (75g) wholemeal flour	¾ cup wholewheat flour
2 size 3 eggs, beaten	2 size 3 eggs, beaten
2 oz (50g) whipping cream *or* 2 oz (50g) low-fat (quark style) soft cheese	2 ounces whipping cream *or* 2 ounces low-fat (quark style) soft cheese

1. Poach the fruit with the water in a covered pan until softened.

2. Purée the fruit and sweeten to taste.

3. Bring the water and margarine to the boil in a heavy-based pan. Remove from the heat.

4. Whisk in the flour to form a soft paste.

5. Return to a gentle heat and continue whisking until the mixture forms a ball that leaves the side of the pan.

6. Remove from the heat and whisk in the egg.

7. Spoon the glossy mixture across two lightly oiled or non-stick bun tins, making 24 in all.

8. Bake in a pre-heated oven at 400°F/200°C (Gas Mark 6) for 20 minutes or until risen, brown and set. *Freeze at this point if desired.*

9. Turn out on to a cooling rack and quickly with a sharp knife make a cut and flap the profiterole open. Return to the oven and dry out a little more.

10. To serve, spoon a little cream or low-fat soft cheese blended with a little of the berry sauce into each shell.

11. Divide across 6 bowls (4 balls in each).

12. Serve with the fruit sauce, cool or slightly warmed as preferred.

Fruit and Nut Round (LF)

(Makes 12 slices)

Total Fibre = 25g
Total Calories = 1380
Total Carbohydrate = 180g
Each piece contains 15g CHO and 115 calories

Imperial (Metric)
5 oz (150g) hazel nuts
3 oz (75g) oats
3 oz (75g) sultanas
3 oz (75g) wholemeal self-raising flour
¼ pint (150ml) unsweetened apple juice

American
5 ounces hazel nuts
¾ cup oats
½ cup golden seedless raisins
¾ cup wholewheat self-raising flour
⅔ cup unsweetened apple juice

1. Lightly roast the hazel nuts in the oven. Remove skins. Divide into 2 equal parts. Finely chop one part and grind the other.

2. Place all the ingredients in a mixing bowl. Mix well.

3. Turn into a non-stick or greased 7-inch (18cm) sandwich tin. Smooth surface.

4. Bake at 350°F/180°C (Gas Mark 4) until brown and firm. Approximately 30-40 minutes.

5. Allow to cool before turning out. *Freezes well.*

6. Yields 12 good slices.

4.

PRESSURE COOKING

Potato and Watercress Soup (LF)

(Serves 4)

Total Fibre = 15g
Total Calories = 400
Total Carbohydrate = 80g
Each serving contains 20g CHO and 100 calories

Imperial (Metric)	**American**
1 lb (450g) potatoes, grated	1 pound potatoes, grated
2 bunches watercress	2 bunches watercress
1 large onion, chopped	1 large onion, chopped
Freshly ground black pepper	Freshly ground black pepper
1 teaspoon sea salt	1 teaspoon sea salt
1 pint (550ml) vegetable stock	2½ cups vegetable stock

1. Place the potatoes in the pressure cooker.

2. Wash watercress, remove any large or tough stalks. Add the watercress, onion, seasoning and stock to the potatoes. Seal the pressure cooker.

3. Bring to pressure and maintain for 10-15 minutes. Reduce pressure.

4. Transfer soup to blender or processor. Blend until the soup is of a smooth consistency. *Freeze at this point if desired.*

5. To serve, warm through gently. Yields 4 good servings. Serve with wholemeal bread or rolls.

Vichy Bean Soup (HF)
Illustrated opposite page 48.
(Serves 6)

Total Fibre = 65g
Total Calories = 720
Total Carbohydrate = 120g
Each serving contains 20g CHO and 120 calories

Imperial (Metric)	American
5 oz (150g) butter beans, soaked	5 ounces Lima beans, soaked
1 lb (450g) carrots, grated	1 pound carrots, grated
1 large onion, chopped	1 large onion, chopped
1 teaspoon sunflower oil	1 teaspoon sunflower oil
1 teaspoon curry powder	1 teaspoon curry powder
1½ pints (825ml) chicken stock	3¾ cups chicken stock
1 oz (25g) raisins	1 ounce raisins

1. Soak the beans in boiling water for 2 hours.

2. Meanwhile, gently sauté the carrot and onion in the oil in the base of the pressure cooker.

3. When softened, add the curry powder, continue cooking for a few minutes and then pour on the stock.

4. Add the drained beans and the raisins. Seal.

5. Bring to full pressure and maintain for 30 minutes. Remove from heat, leave to reduce pressure.

6. Transfer the soup to a liquidizer or processor. Blend to a smooth consistency. *Freeze at this point if desired.*

7. Reheat gently, stirring continuously. Serve with a spoonful of plain yogurt and chopped parsley.

Cream of Onion Soup (LF)

(Serves 4)

Total Fibre = 15g
Total Calories = 740
Total Carbohydrate = 100g
Each serving contains 25g CHO and 185 calories

Imperial (Metric)	**American**
1 oz (25g) sunflower margarine	2½ tablespoons margarine
2 lbs (900g) onion, finely chopped	2 pounds onion, finely chopped
1 potato (4 oz/100g), peeled, diced	1 potato (4 ounce), peeled and diced
1 pint (550ml) skimmed milk	2½ cups skimmed milk
1 teaspoon marjoram	1 teaspoon marjoram
Freshly ground black pepper	Freshly ground black pepper
Sea salt	Sea salt
3 tablespoons wholemeal flour	3 tablespoons wholewheat flour

1. Melt the margarine in the pressure cooker. Add the onion. Cover and 'sweat' in the covered pan for about 5 minutes. Allow onion to brown slightly.

2. Add the potato, milk, marjoram and seasoning. Seal and cook under pressure for 5 minutes. Reduce pressure, remove lid and stir in the flour. Cook over a low heat for 5 minutes.

3. Blend or process until smooth. *Freeze at this point if desired.*

4. Adjust seasoning. To serve, reheat gently. If too thick, dilute with vegetable stock.

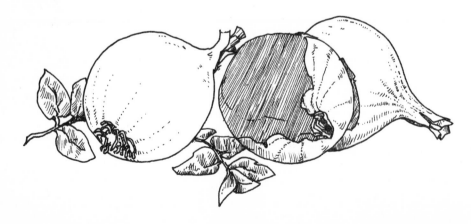

West Country Pâté (LF)

(Serves 6-8)

Total Fibre = 5g
Total Calories = 1020
Total Carbohydrate = 40g
Each serving provides 5g CHO and 130-170 calories

Imperial (Metric)	American
½ oz (15g) sunflower margarine	1 tablespoon sunflower margarine
1 medium onion, diced	1 medium onion, diced
1 clove of garlic, finely sliced	1 clove of garlic, finely sliced
1 lb (450g) pig's liver, cubed	1 pound pig's liver, cubed
1 bay leaf	1 bay leaf
¼ pint (150ml) medium dry cider	⅔ cup medium dry cider
1 tablespoon tomato purée	1 tablespoon tomato paste
Freshly ground black pepper	Freshly ground black pepper
½ teaspoon thyme	½ teaspoon thyme
3 oz (75g) fresh wholemeal breadcrumbs	1½ cups fresh wholewheat breadcrumbs

1. Sweat the onion and garlic in the margarine in the base of the pressure cooker for a minute or two.

2. Add the liver to the pot and brown. Stir in the bay leaf and cider.

3. Cover and simmer for 5 minutes.

4. Add the tomato purée (paste), pepper and thyme. Seal and hold under high pressure for 10 minutes.

5. Reduce pressure, add the breadcrumbs.

6. Then pass through a coarse sieve or blend or process to a smooth paste.

7. Place in a serving dish, smooth the top and cover with greaseproof paper. Place a plate and a weight on top and leave in the fridge for at least 4 hours before serving. *Freeze at this point if desired.*

8. Before serving with wholemeal toast fingers or wholemeal crisp rolls, garnish with a little mustard and cress and sliced tomatoes.

Lentil Warmer (HF)

(Serves 4 as main course or 8 as a starter)

Total Fibre = 50g
Total Calories = 880
Total Carbohydrate = 160g
Each serving contains 40g (or 20g) CHO and 220 (or 110) calories

Imperial (Metric)	**American**
8 oz (225g) orange lentils	1 cup orange lentils
1 lb (450g) white cabbage, sliced	1 pound white cabbage, sliced
1 large onion, sliced	1 large onion, sliced
8 oz (225g) carrot, sliced	8 ounces carrot, sliced
2 pints (1.1l) vegetable stock	5 cups vegetable stock
1 teaspoon caraway seeds	1 teaspoon caraway seeds
½ teaspoon sea salt	½ teaspoon sea salt
Freshly ground black pepper	Freshly ground black pepper

1. Rinse the lentils in cold water and drain.

2. Place all the ingredients in the pressure cooker and seal.

3. Bring to the boil and put under pressure, then cook under full pressure for 15 minutes.

4. Remove from heat and leave to cool.

5. When cool, liquidize or process. *Freeze at this point if desired.*

6. To serve, warm through gently, stirring continuously.

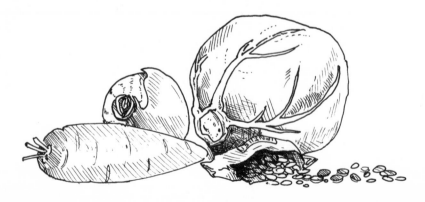

Brown Rice (LF)
'So quick there's no excuse not to try it'

(4 modest servings)

Total Fibre = 10g
Total Calories = 800
Total Carbohydrate = 160g
Each serving contains 40g CHO and 200 calories

Imperial (Metric)	**American**
8 oz (225g) brown rice, washed	1 cup brown rice
2 pints (1.1l) boiling water	5 cups boiling water
½-1 teaspoon sea salt	½-1 teaspoon sea salt

1. Place the rice, water and salt in the pressure cooker. Secure lid.

2. Bring to pressure. Hold at full pressure for 10 minutes.

3. Remove from the heat, reduce pressure and remove lid.

4. Strain the rice. Leave in the sieve and dry over the heat for a minute or two before serving.

Note: It is worth cooking extra rice and storing in the fridge for use in salads etc. Brown rice doubles its weight when cooked by this method. Allow about 50g CHO for every 5 oz (150g) of cooked rice.

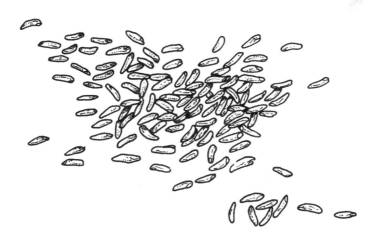

Pork and Pasta Pudding (LF)

(Serves 4)

Total Fibre = 10g
Total Calories = 1060
Total Carbohydrate = 60g
Each serving contains 15g CHO and 265 calories

Imperial (Metric)	**American**
3 oz (75g) wholewheat macaroni	3 ounces wholewheat macaroni
½ pint (275ml) salted water	1⅓ cups salted water
1 lb (450g) lean minced pork	1 pound lean minced pork
1 clove garlic, crushed	1 clove garlic, crushed
1 small onion, chopped	1 small onion, chopped
1 small red pepper, diced	1 small red pepper, diced
1×14 oz (400g) tin chopped tomatoes	1×14 ounce can chopped tomatoes
1 tablespoon tomato purée	1 tablespoon tomato paste
1 size 3 egg, beaten	1 size 3 egg, beaten
1 teaspoon thyme	1 teaspoon thyme
1 teaspoon tarragon	1 teaspoon tarragon
Freshly ground black pepper	Freshly ground black pepper
1 teaspoon soya sauce	1 teaspoon soy sauce

1. Cook the macaroni in the water under full pressure for 5-7 minutes.

2. Meanwhile brown the pork, without added fat, in a heavy-based pan. Drain off any fat.

3. Combine the pork with the remaining ingredients.

4. Drain the pasta well. Mix with the other ingredients.

5. Transfer to 2 pint (1.1l) pudding basin. Smooth the top and cover securely with foil.

6. Cook under full pressure for 15 minutes.

7. Serve with green vegetables, sweetcorn and bread.

Midweek Casserole (MF)
'A creamy combination of parsnip and beans'

(Serves 4)

Total Fibre = 35g
Total Calories = 1240
Total Carbohydrate = 120g
Each serving contains 30g CHO and 310 calories

Imperial (Metric)	American
5 oz (150g) borlotti beans	5 ounces pinto beans
1 lb (450g) scrag or neck of lamb	1 pound scrag or neck of lamb
1 pint (550ml) water	2½ cups water
1 bay leaf	1 bay leaf
1 large parsnip, sliced	1 large parsnip, sliced
1 medium onion, sliced	1 medium onion, sliced
2 tablespoons wholemeal flour	2 tablespoons wholewheat flour
1 tablespoon tomato purée	1 tablespoon tomato paste
½ teaspoon rosemary	½ teaspoon rosemary
Freshly ground black pepper	Freshly ground black pepper
Sea salt	Sea salt

1. Soak the beans in boiling water. Cover and leave for 2 hours or overnight.

2. Put the lamb, water and bay leaf in the pressure cooker. Seal and cook under pressure for 15 minutes.

3. Reduce pressure and leave in a cool place to go quite cold. Remove the lid, skim off any solid fat. With a draining spoon remove meat to a plate. Cover.

4. Drain and rinse the beans. Transfer to the pressure cooker. Bring to the boil and hold for 10 minutes. Then seal and cook under pressure in the meat stock for 10-15 minutes.

5. Reduce pressure, add the meat and all the vegetables.

6. Mix the flour, tomato purée (paste) and a little water to a paste. Stir into the meat and vegetables.

7. Add the herbs and seasoning. Seal and cook under pressure for 5 minutes. *Freeze at this point if desired.* Serve with wholemeal or granary bread.

Steak and Mushroom Pudding (LF)

(Serves 2)

Total Fibre = 5g
Total Calories = 800
Total Carbohydrate = 60g
Each serving contains 30g CHO and 400 calories

Filling:

Imperial (Metric)	**American**
8 oz (225g) lean stewing beef, cubed	8 ounces lean stewing beef, cubed
½ small onion, sliced	½ small onion, sliced
1 small bay leaf	1 small bay leaf
½ teaspoon thyme	½ teaspoon thyme
¼ pint (150ml) strong beef stock	⅔ cup strong beef stock
1 tablespoon tomato purée	1 tablespoon tomato paste
4 oz (100g) field mushrooms, sliced	4 ounces field mushrooms, sliced
Freshly ground black pepper	Freshly ground black pepper

Pastry:

Imperial (Metric)	**American**
3 oz (75g) wholemeal flour	¾ cup wholewheat flour
1 teaspoon baking powder	1 teaspoon baking powder
1 oz (25g) sunflower margarine	2½ tablespoons sunflower margarine
Cold water	Cold water

1. Place the beef, onion, herbs and stock in the pressure cooker.

2. Seal and cook under high pressure for 15 minutes.

3. Reduce the pressure, remove the lid and stir in the tomato purée (paste).

4. Add the mushrooms and season with the pepper, then turn into a 1 pint (550ml) basin.

5. Place the flour and baking powder in a small bowl. Rub in the margarine and bind together with a little cold water.

6. Shape the dough to fit the top of the basin, cover with pleated greaseproof and cover with foil securely.

7. Place in a pressure cooker with enough water to reach at least ⅓ of the way up the basin. Replace lid but do not seal.

8. Place on a moderate heat and maintain for 5 minutes (steam should be coming out of the vent).

9. Put under pressure, reduce heat a little and cook for a further 10 minutes. Allow to reduce pressure slowly.

10. To serve divide into 2 and serve with green beans and cauliflower. *Do not freeze.*

Pineapple Pudding (LF)

(Serves 4)

Total Fibre = 15g
Total Calories = 720
Total Carbohydrate = 80g
Each serving contains 20g CHO and 180 calories

Imperial (Metric)	American
2 slices (about 4 oz/100g) pineapple in natural juice, chopped	2 slices (about 4 ounces) pineapple in natural juice, chopped
⅛ pint (75ml) reserved pineapple juice	¼ cup reserved pineapple juice
2 large slices medium-cut wholemeal bread, crumbed	2 large slices medium-cut wholewheat bread, crumbed
2 tablespoons ground almonds	2 tablespoons ground almonds
1 oz (25g) flaked almonds	¼ cup slivered almonds
2 oz (50g) porridge oats	½ cup rolled oats
½ teaspoon mixed spice	½ teaspoon mixed spice
1 size 3 egg, beaten	1 size 3 egg, beaten

1. Mix all the ingredients together. Cover and leave to stand for half an hour.

2. If the mixture is very stiff add a few spoons of skimmed milk.

3. Press the mixture into a lightly oiled 1 pint (550ml) bowl. Cover securely with foil.

4. Transfer to the pressure cooker. Add sufficient water to reach half-way up the bowl. Seal. Bring to pressure and hold at full pressure for 20 minutes.

5. Remove from heat and allow to reduce pressure gradually.

6. Turn out and cut into 4. Serve with a little custard or evaporated milk. *Do not freeze.*

Pressure Cooked Pudding (MF)

(Serves 6)

Total Fibre = 25g
Total Calories = 1050
Total Carbohydrate = 180g
Each serving contains 30g CHO and 175 calories

Imperial (Metric)	**American**
¼ pint (150ml) skimmed milk	⅔ cup skimmed milk
3 oz (75g) dried dates, finely chopped	½ cup finely chopped dried dates
3 oz (75g) raisins or sultanas	½ cup golden seedless raisins
3 oz (75g) self-raising wholemeal flour	¾ cup self-raising wholewheat flour
1 teaspoon baking powder	1 teaspoon baking powder
1 teaspoon mixed spice	1 teaspoon mixed spice
2 oz (50g) fresh wholemeal breadcrumbs	1 cup fresh wholewheat breadcrumbs
2 tablespoons sunflower oil	2 tablespoons sunflower oil
Juice and rind of 1 large orange	Juice and rind of 1 large orange

1. Simmer the milk with the dates and raisins for 5 minutes. Leave to cool.

2. Place the remaining ingredients in a mixing bowl. Mix well. Pour on the cooled milk and fruit mixture. Beat well.

3. Turn the mixture into a lightly oiled 1 pint (550ml) pudding basin and cover securely with greaseproof and foil.

4. Place in pressure cooker. Boil for 5 minutes before bringing to full pressure, then cook under full pressure for 30 minutes.

5. Remove from heat and allow to reduce pressure normally before removing. *Freeze at this point if desired.*

6. Serve hot with a little evaporated milk or allow to cool and serve slices with a little unsweetened fruit.

Rice Condé (LF)

(Serves 4)

Total Fibre = 5g
Total Calories = 540
Total Carbohydrate = 80g
Each serving contains 20g CHO and 135 calories

Imperial (Metric)	**American**
3 oz (75g) short grain brown rice	3 ounces short grain brown rice
¼ pint (150ml) water	⅔ cup water
2 size 3 eggs, beaten	2 size 3 eggs, beaten
½ pint (275ml) skimmed milk	1⅓ cups skimmed milk
2 tablespoons dried fruit	2 tablespoons dried fruit
½ teaspoon cinnamon	½ teaspoon cinnamon
2-3 drops vanilla flavouring	2-3 drops vanilla flavouring
Liquid or non-nutritive powder sweetener to taste	Liquid or non-nutritive powder sweetener to taste

1. Cook the rice in the water under full pressure for 15 minutes. Drain well and cool slightly.

2. Whisk the remaining ingredients together.

3. Mix the softened rice and egg mixture together.

4. Pour into a lightly oiled 1 pint (550ml) pudding basin. Cover securely with foil.

5. Cook under full pressure for 10 minutes. Allow to reduce pressure gradually.

6. When pressure is reduced remove the basin from the cooker. Allow to cool before serving.

7. Alternatively — spend an extra moment or two to purée the mixture using a blender, food processor or sieve. Adjust sweetening if necessary.

8. Serve with stewed fruit.

5.

SLOW COOKING

Pot Cod (LF)

(Serves 2)

Total Fibre = 5g
Total Calories = 460
Total Carbohydrate = 20g
Each serving contains 10g CHO and 230 calories

Imperial (Metric)	American
1 large onion, sliced	1 large onion, sliced
1 large red pepper, chopped	1 large red pepper, chopped
6 oz (175g) carrots, diced	1 cup carrots, diced
1 lb (450g) cod fillet	1 pound cod fillet
1 teaspoon mixed herbs	1 teaspoon mixed herbs
Freshly ground black pepper	Freshly ground black pepper
A pinch of sea salt	A pinch of sea salt
½ pint (275ml) hot fish stock	1⅓ cups hot fish stock
1 tablespoon tomato purée	1 tablespoon tomato paste
Chopped parsley for garnish	Chopped parsley for garnish

1. Place the onion, pepper and carrots in the pre-heated slow cooker.

2. Cut the fish into strips, sprinkle with the herbs, pepper and salt.

3. Transfer to slow cooker. Pour over the fish stock. Stir in the tomato purée (paste). Cover.

4. Cook on LOW for about 8-10 hours.

5. Sprinkle with the parsley and serve with creamed potatoes, whole green beans and a little sweetcorn.

Caraway Chicken (LF)

(Serves 4)

Total Fibre = 15g
Total Calories = 960
Total Carbohydrate = 15g
Each serving contains negligible CHO and 240 calories

Imperial (Metric)	**American**
4 chicken joints, 2 lb/900g total	4 chicken joints, 2 pounds in total
1 tablespoon caraway seeds	1 tablespoon caraway seeds
1 lb (450g) winter cabbage, sliced	1 pound winter cabbage, sliced
1 medium onion, chopped	1 medium onion, chopped
Freshly ground black pepper	Freshly ground black pepper
Sea salt	Sea salt
¾ pint (425ml) chicken stock, hot	2 cups chicken stock, hot
6 oz (175g) sweetcorn, tinned or frozen	1 cup sweetcorn, canned or frozen

1. Trim off any visible fat and most of the skin from the chicken joints. Sprinkle over the caraway seeds and leave to one side while the slow cooker is heating up.

2. When the slow cooker is hot (approx. 20 minutes) cover the bottom of the cooker with the cabbage. Place the joints on the cabbage bed. Sprinkle over onion and seasoning. Pour over the hot stock. Cover.

3. Cook on HIGH for 5 hours *or* 1 hour on HIGH and 6-8 hours on LOW.

4. *Freeze at this point if desired.* Before serving stir in the hot corn. Brown in a hot oven if desired. Serve with green vegetables and wholemeal bread or jacket potatoes.

Beef 'n Beans (MF)

(Serves 4)

Total Fibre = 20g
Total Calories = 960
Total Carbohydrate = 60g
Each serving contains 15g CHO and 240 calories

Imperial (Metric)
1 medium red pepper, chopped
1 large onion, chopped
1×15 oz (425g) tin butter beans, drained
1×14 oz (400g) tin chopped tomatoes
1 lb (450g) lean stewing beef, trimmed and cubed
1 teaspoon paprika
¼ pint (150ml) hot beef stock
Sea salt to taste

American
1 medium red pepper, chopped
1 large onion, chopped
1×15 ounce can Lima beans, drained
1×14 ounce can chopped tomatoes
1 pound lean stewing beef, trimmed and cubed
1 teaspoon paprika
⅔ cup hot beef stock
Sea salt to taste

1. Place the pepper, onion and drained beans in the pre-heated slow cooker.

2. Mix the beef and tomatoes together. Turn into the slow cooker.

3. Sprinkle over the paprika.

4. Pour over the stock. Add the sea salt.

5. Cook on LOW for 8-10 hours *or* 4-5 hours on HIGH. *Freeze at this point if desired.*

6. Serve with wholewheat noodles or jacket potatoes and a green vegetable.

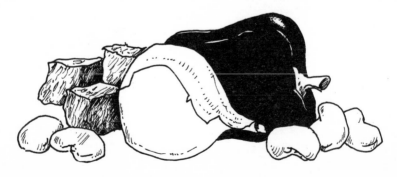

Cabbage Packages (LF)

Illustrated opposite page 49.
(Serves 4)

Total Fibre = 15g
Total Calories = 800
Total Carbohydrate = 80g
Each serving contains 20g CHO and 200 calories

Imperial (Metric)	**American**
8 large or 12 small cabbage leaves	8 large or 12 small cabbage leaves
8 oz (225g) lean minced beef	8 ounces ground beef
3 oz (75g) brown long grain rice	3 ounces brown long grain rice
¾ pint (425ml) beef stock	2 cups beef stock
1 medium onion, chopped	1 medium onion, chopped
1 lb (450g) tomatoes, skinned and pulped	1 pound tomatoes, skinned and pulped
1 teaspoon dried mixed herbs	1 teaspoon dried mixed herbs
A good pinch of paprika	A good pinch of paprika
Freshly ground black pepper	Freshly ground black pepper
Sea salt (optional)	Sea salt (optional)
1 tablespoon tomato purée	1 tablespoon tomato paste

1. Soften the whole cabbage leaves in boiling water. Drain.

2. Brown the minced beef in a heavy pan. Transfer to a mixing bowl. Simmer the rice in the stock with the onion until slightly softened. Drain, retaining the stock. Transfer to the mixing bowl.

3. Add the tomatoes, herbs, spice and seasoning. Mix well.

4. Divide the mixture across the cabbage leaves. Fold into packets. Place in the pre-heated slow cooker.

5. Mix the tomato purée (paste) with the retained stock. Bring back to boiling point. Pour over packets.

6. Cover and cook on HIGH for 4 hours *or* HIGH for 1 hour followed by 6-8 hours on LOW. *Freeze at this point if desired.*

7. Serve with green beans and jacket potatoes.

Beef Curry (MF)

(Serves 6)

Total Fibre = 30g
Total Calories = 1740
Total Carbohydrate = 150g
Each serving contains 25g CHO and 290 calories

Imperial (Metric)	**American**
3 oz (75g) green lentils	3 ounces green lentils
1 tablespoon sunflower oil	1 tablespoon sunflower oil
1¼ lbs (600g) lean beef, cubed	1¼ pounds lean beef, cubed
1 teaspoon ground ginger	1 teaspoon ground ginger
2-3 teaspoons Madras (hot) curry powder	2-3 teaspoons Madras (hot) curry powder
1 teaspoon garam masala	1 teaspoon garam masala
1 teaspoon ground coriander	1 teaspoon ground coriander
4-5 pieces dried chilli	4-5 pieces dried chili
Sea salt	Sea salt
1 large onion, chopped	1 large onion, chopped
1 lb (450g) carrots, sliced	1 pound carrots, sliced
12 oz (350g) potatoes, cubed	12 ounces potatoes, cubed
1½ pints (850ml) beef stock	3¾ cups beef stock
1 tablespoon tomato purée	1 tablespoon tomato paste

1. Boil the lentils for about 10 minutes. Drain well.

2. Meanwhile heat the oil in a large heavy-based pan or frying pan.

3. Mix the meat and seasonings together. Add to the hot oil, continue heating until the meat is brown. Add the onion and continue cooking for 2-3 minutes.

4. Add the carrots, drained lentils, potatoes, stock and tomato purée (paste). Bring to the boil and simmer for 5 minutes.

5. Turn into pre-heated slow cooker. Cook on HIGH for 4 hours then on LOW for 8 hours. *Freeze at this point if desired.*

6. Serve with boiled brown rice and whole green beans.

Convenience Pork (MF)

(Serves 4)

Total Fibre = 20g
Total Calories = 1360
Total Carbohydrate = 100g
Each serving contains 25g CHO and 340 calories

Imperial (Metric)	**American**
1 lb (450g) lean stewing pork, cubed	1 pound lean stewing pork, cubed
1 teaspoon caraway seeds	1 teaspoon caraway seeds
1 small onion, chopped	1 small onion, chopped
¼ pint (150ml) dry white wine	¾ cup dry white wine
1 large red pepper, sliced	1 large red pepper, sliced
1 stick of celery, sliced	1 celery stalk, sliced
1×15 oz (425g) tin chick peas, drained	1×15 ounce can garbanzo beans, drained
1 packet (50g) Chicken Chasseur Sauce Mix	1 packet Chicken Chasseur Sauce Mix
½ pint (275ml) water	1⅓ cups water
Freshly ground black pepper	Freshly ground black pepper

1. Place the pork, caraway seeds and onion in a heavy-based pan. Brown without added fat.

2. Pour over the wine, cover and simmer for 5 minutes.

3. Meanwhile place the pepper, celery and drained chick peas (garbanzos) in the pre-heated slow cooker.

4. Blend the sauce mix with a little of the cold water to form a paste. Add the remaining water. Stir into the pork and wine mixture. Bring to the boil. Season with black pepper.

5. Turn the pork into the pre-heated slow cooker. Cover and cook on HIGH for 6-8 hours. *Freeze at this point if desired.* Reheat thoroughly before serving.

6. Serve green vegetables or cauliflower and wholewheat noodles or jacket potatoes.

Lamb in the Pot (LF)
'A quick to prepare midweek meal'

(Serves 2)

Total Fibre = 5g
Total Calories = 580
Total Carbohydrate = negligible
Each serving contains negligible CHO and 290 calories

Imperial (Metric)
1 medium onion, sliced
½ lb (225g) winter cabbage, sliced
   thinly
1 medium red pepper, diced
4 small lamb cutlets
or 10 oz (275g) lean boned stewing
   lamb
1 teaspoon Worcester sauce
1 teaspoon soya sauce
Freshly ground black pepper
¾ pint (425ml) vegetable stock,
   boiling

American
1 medium onion, sliced
2 cups shredded winter cabbage
1 medium red pepper, diced
4 small lamb cutlets
or 10 ounces lean boned stewing
   lamb
1 teaspoon Worcester sauce
1 teaspoon soy sauce
Freshly ground black pepper
2 cups vegetable stock, boiling

1. Place the onion, winter cabbage and red pepper in the pre-heated slow cooker.

2. Trim off all the visible fat from the lamb cutlets.

3. Place on top of the vegetables, sprinkle over the Worcester and soya sauce.
    Season with black pepper.

4. Pour over the boiling vegetable stock. Cover and cook on LOW for 8-10 hours.
    Do not freeze.

5. Serve with swede and creamed potatoes.

Mustard Lamb (LF)

(Serves 4)

Total Fibre = 5g
Total Calories = 1000
Total Carbohydrate = 40g
Each serving contains 10g CHO and 250 calories

Imperial (Metric)	**American**
1 lb (450g) lamb's liver, cubed	1 pound lamb's liver, cubed
1 teaspoon paprika	1 teaspoon paprika
2 teaspoons French mustard	2 teaspoons French mustard
Plenty of freshly ground black pepper	Plenty of freshly ground black pepper
1 teaspoon sunflower oil	1 teaspoon sunflower oil
1 tablespoon wholemeal flour	1 tablespoon wholewheat flour
¼ pint (150ml) vegetable stock	⅔ cup vegetable stock
1 large onion, chopped	1 large onion, chopped
1 large carrot, finely chopped	1 large carrot, finely chopped
1 medium parsnip, finely chopped	1 medium parsnip, finely chopped
A pinch of sea salt	A pinch of sea salt

1. Mix the liver, paprika, mustard and pepper together.

2. Heat the oil in a small heavy-based pan. Add the liver, continue cooking stirring occasionally, until brown and sealed. Add the flour and stock. Bring to the boil then simmer for 2-3 minutes.

3. Meanwhile place the vegetables in the pre-heated slow cooker.

4. Add the liver and stock, sprinkle over the sea salt, mix well and cover.

5. Cook on HIGH for about 4 hours *or* LOW for 7 hours. *Freeze at this point if desired.*

6. Serve with wholewheat tagliatelle and green vegetables.

Slo Xmas Pud (MF)
'Rich and fruity'

(Serves 8)

Total Fibre = 50g
Total Calories = 2320
Total Carbohydrate = 240g
Each serving contains 30g CHO and 290 calories

Imperial (Metric)	American
3 oz (75g) self-raising wholemeal flour	¾ cup self-raising wholewheat flour
3 oz (75g) fresh wholemeal breadcrumbs	1½ cups fresh wholewheat breadcrumbs
5 oz (150g) raisins	5 ounces raisins
3 oz (75g) sultanas	½ cup golden seedless raisins
2 oz (50g) ground almonds	½ cup ground almonds
3 oz (75g) flaked almonds	¾ cup slivered almonds
2 tablespoons fruit sugar (fructose)	2 tablespoons fruit sugar (fructose)
½ teaspoon mixed spice	½ teaspoon mixed spice
½ teaspoon cinnamon	½ teaspoon cinnamon
½ teaspoon nutmeg	½ teaspoon nutmeg
8 oz (225g) carrots, grated or finely chopped	8 ounces carrots, grated or finely chopped
Grated rind and juice of a large orange	Grated rind and juice of a large orange
2 size 3 eggs, beaten	2 size 3 eggs, beaten
2 tablespoons sunflower oil	2 tablespoons sunflower oil
2 tablespoons brandy	2 tablespoons brandy

1. Put all the dry ingredients in a large mixing bowl.

2. Add the carrot, rind, juice, egg, oil and brandy. Mix well.

3. Transfer to a lightly oiled 2 pint (1.1l) basin. Cover with greaseproof and secure with foil.

4. Place in a pre-heated slow cooker. Pour in sufficient hot water to come two-thirds up the side of the basin. Replace lid. Cook on HIGH for 11-12 hours.

5. Remove and allow to go quite cold. Wrap securely and freeze. (Keeps well for up to 6 weeks.)

6. To serve, reheat either in a pressure-cooker, microwave or pre-heated slow cooker on HIGH for about 4 hours.

Coconut Custard (LF)

(Serves 4)

Total Fibre = 5g
Total Calories = 480
Total Carbohydrate = 20g
Each serving contains 5g CHO and 120 calories

Imperial (Metric)
3 tablespoons desiccated coconut
½ pint (275ml) skimmed milk
1 tablespoon sultanas
½ teaspoon vanilla flavouring
2 size 3 eggs plus 1 size 3 egg yolk,
  beaten together
Nutmeg
Liquid or non-nutritive powder
  sweetener to taste (optional)

American
3 tablespoons desiccated coconut
1⅓ cups skimmed milk
1 tablespoon golden seedless raisins
½ teaspoon vanilla flavouring
2 size 3 eggs plus 1 size 3 egg yolk,
  beaten together
Nutmeg
Liquid or non-nutritive powder
  sweetener to taste (optional)

1. Warm the coconut, milk and sultanas (golden seedless raisins) together. Add the vanilla flavouring.

2. Pour the warm milk onto the beaten eggs. Whisk well.

3. Pour into a lightly oiled 1 pint (550ml) pudding basin. Sprinkle with nutmeg. Stir in sweetener if needed. Cover with foil.

4. Place in a pre-heated slow cooker. Add sufficient boiling water to reach half way up the basin.

5. Cover and cook on LOW for 3-4 hours.

6. Allow to cool or go quite cold before turning out and serving.

Slo-Rice Pudding (LF)

(Serves 4)

Total Fibre = 5g
Total Calories = 520
Total Carbohydrate = 100g
Each serving contains 25g CHO and 130 calories

Imperial (Metric)
3 oz (75g) short grain brown rice
¼ pint (150ml) water
1 pint (550ml) skimmed milk
1 oz (25g) sultanas
1 teaspoon ground nutmeg or
  cinnamon

American
3 ounces short grain brown rice
⅔ cup water
2½ cups skimmed milk
1 ounce golden seedless raisins
1 teaspoon ground nutmeg or
  cinnamon

1. To soften the rice bring to the boil in the water. Simmer for 10-15 minutes.

2. Turn into pre-heated and lightly greased slow cooker.

3. Add milk, sultanas (golden seedless raisins) and spice of choice. Cover.

4. Cook on LOW for 6-8 hours.

5. Serve hot or cold. *Do not freeze.*

Citrus Marmalade

(Makes 6-6.5 lbs)

Total Calories = 5800
Total Carbohydrate = 120g
1 oz provides negligible CHO and 60 calories

Imperial (Metric)
5 lbs (2.30kg) seville oranges,
  washed
2 large lemons, washed and dried
4 pints (2.2 litres) boiling water
3 lbs (1.50kg) fruit sugar (fructose),
  warmed in oven

American
5 pounds seville oranges, washed
2 large lemons, washed and dried
10 cups boiling water
3 pounds fruit sugar (fructose),
  warmed in oven

1. With a very sharp knife or potato peeler remove the rind (not the white pith) from the oranges and lemons.

2. Squeeze the oranges and lemons. Retain the pips.

3. Place the strained juice with the rind and 2 pints of the water in the pre-heated slow cooker. Cook on LOW for 8-10 hours.

4. Finely chop (or process) the pith and flesh of the fruit in a large pan. Add the pips and the remaining water and simmer for at least 1 hour. Allow to cool slightly.

5. Strain into a fresh large pan. Cover and leave until the peel is ready.

6. Add the peel mixture to the large pan. Add the warmed fruit sugar. Heat gently stirring continuously while the fruit sugar dissolves.

7. Turn up the heat, boil rapidly until the marmalade thickens.

8. To test for set, use a thermometer (220°F/104°C) or place a teaspoon of the marmalade on a cold plate — if a weak skin forms, the marmalade will make a soft set.

9. Allow to cool before pouring into hot, clean jam jars. Seal and label.

10. Store in a cool, dry area.

Notes: This method will give a soft setting marmalade which spreads well but not thickly. If a harder set is required, more fruit sugar could be used, but this will increase the cost of the final product. An alternative is to add 2 or 3 sachets of gelatine to the jam while it is still hot.

*   The carbohydrate contribution from the fructose has been ignored as usual — but remember each ounce of the final product will provide approximately 15g of fruit sugar.

6.

QUICK AND CONVENIENT

Quick Beans (MF)

'A quick and tasty snack meal'
Illustrated opposite page 81.
(Serves 2)

Total Fibre = 15g
Total Calories = 420
Total Carbohydrate = 60g
Each serving contains 30g CHO and 210 calories

Imperial (Metric)	American
1 medium onion, chopped	1 medium onion, chopped
4 large tomatoes, chopped	4 large tomatoes, chopped
1 teaspoon sunflower oil	1 teaspoon sunflower oil
1×15 oz (425g) tin of butter beans, drained	1×15 ounce can of Lima beans, drained
1 teaspoon oregano	1 teaspoon oregano
Fresh basil	Fresh basil
Freshly ground black pepper	Freshly ground black pepper
Sea salt	Sea salt

1. Place the onion, tomatoes and oil in a heavy pan. Cover and simmer gently for 5-10 minutes.

2. Add the beans and herbs. Season well. Cover pan again and heat through thoroughly.

3. Serve with wholemeal pittas or bread.

Soup in a Hurry (HF)

(Serves 4)

Total Fibre = 40g
Total Calories = 720
Total Carbohydrate = 120g
Each serving contains 30g CHO and 180 calories

Imperial (Metric)
1 large onion, finely chopped
1 teaspoon sunflower oil
1×15½ oz (440g) tin chick peas,
  rinsed and drained
1×11½ oz (330g) tin sweetcorn
1×14 oz (400g) tin chopped
  tomatoes
1 teaspoon dried basil
1 teaspoon vegetable extract
1 teaspoon tomato purée
1 pint (550ml) water
Freshly ground black pepper
Sea salt

American
1 large onion, finely chopped
1 teaspoon sunflower oil
1×15½ ounce can garbanzo beans,
  rinsed and drained
2 cups canned sweetcorn
1×14 ounce can chopped tomatoes
1 teaspoon dried basil
1 teaspoon vegetable extract
1 teaspoon tomato paste
2½ cups water
Freshly ground black pepper
Sea salt

1. Gently cook the onion in oil in a covered pan.

2. When the onions are brown add the remaining ingredients. Mix well.

3. Cover and bring to the boil. Reduce heat and simmer for approximately 10 minutes.

4. Liquidize or process till smooth. *Freeze at this point if desired.*

5. Return to the heat, adjust seasoning (thin down with extra vegetable stock if required). Serve with wholemeal or granary rolls for a quick and filling meal.

Prawns in Nut Sauce (LF)

Illustrated opposite page 81.
(Serves 2)

Total Fibre = negligible
Total Calories = 480
Total Carbohydrate = 10g
Each serving contains 5g CHO and 240 calories

Imperial (Metric)	**American**
1 teaspoon sunflower oil	1 teaspoon sunflower oil
1 small onion, chopped	1 small onion, chopped
1 medium red pepper, sliced	1 medium red pepper, sliced
2 tablespoons crunchy peanut butter	2 tablespoons crunchy peanut butter
⅛ pint (75ml) tomato juice	⅓ cup tomato juice
2-3 drops soya sauce	2-3 drops soy sauce
1 small tin (7 oz/200g) prawns in brine, drained	1 small can (7 ounce) prawns in brine, drained
or 6 oz (175g) cooked prawns	*or* 6 ounces cooked prawns
Freshly ground black pepper	Freshly ground black pepper

1. Heat the oil in a small heavy-based pan. Add the onion and pepper, cover and sauté gently.

2. Stir in the peanut butter, tomato juice and soya sauce, reduce heat and continue cooking for 2-3 minutes.

3. Add the prawns. Simmer until thoroughly heated through. *Freeze at this point if desired.*

4. Serve on a bed of boiled wholewheat pasta (shells or tagliatelle) with whole green beans and sweetcorn.

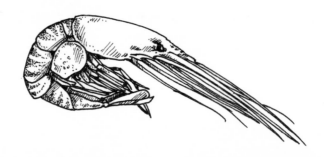

Pilchard Bake (LF)

(Serves 4)

Total Fibre = negligible
Total Calories = 880
Total Carbohydrate = 10g
Each serving contains negligible CHO and 220 calories

Imperial (Metric)

1×15 oz (425g) tin pilchards in
  brine, drained
1 small tin chopped tomatoes
Freshly ground black pepper
4 size 3 eggs, whisked
¼ pint (150ml) skimmed milk
1 teaspoon mixed dried herbs

American

1×15 ounce can pilchards in brine,
  drained
1 small can chopped tomatoes
Freshly ground black pepper
4 size 3 eggs, whisked
⅔ cup skimmed milk
1 teaspoon mixed dried herbs

1. Flake the fish and mix with the tomatoes. Season well.

2. Mix the whisked eggs, milk and herbs together.

3. Combine the fish and egg mixtures. Pour into a non-stick or lightly oiled ovenproof dish.

4. Cook at 350°F/180°C (Gas Mark 4) for 30 minutes or until browned and set.

5. Serve immediately with jacket or creamed potatoes and green vegetables.

Vegetable and Tuna Medley (MF)

(Serves 2)

Total Fibre = 15g
Total Calories = 720
Total Carbohydrate = 70g
Each serving contains 35g CHO and 360 calories

Imperial (Metric)
1 tablespoon sunflower oil
1 large onion, chopped
1 medium green pepper, sliced
8 oz (225g) cooked potatoes, cubed
4 oz (100g) cup mushrooms, sliced
1×15 oz (425g) tin broad beans,
 drained
1×7oz (200g) tin tuna in brine,
 drained and flaked
1 tablespoon tomato purée
1 teaspoon paprika
¼ pint (150ml) boiling water

American
1 tablespoon sunflower oil
1 large onion, chopped
1 medium green pepper, sliced
8 ounces cooked potatoes, cubed
4 ounces cup mushrooms, sliced
1×15 ounce can fava beans, drained
1×7 ounce can tuna in brine,
 drained and flaked
1 tablespoon tomato paste
1 teaspoon paprika
⅔ cup boiling water

1. Heat the oil in a heavy-based pan.

2. Add the onion and pepper and sauté gently.

3. Add the potato, mushrooms and beans, and heat gently.

4. Stir in the tuna.

5. Mix the tomato purée (paste), paprika and boiling water together. Pour over the mixture in the pan. Cover and continue cooking for 10 minutes until thoroughly heated through.

6. Serve with boiled brown rice or wholewheat pitta breads and green beans. *Do not freeze.*

Opposite: Simple yet sophisticated, Cool Raspberry Mould (page 92).

Kipper Kedgeree (MF)
Illustrated opposite.
(Serves 2-3)

Total Fibre = 15g
Total Calories = 1100
Total Carbohydrate = 120g
Each serving (if 2) contains 60g CHO and 550 calories
                (if 3) contains 40g CHO and 365 calories

Imperial (Metric)	**American**
5 oz (150g) brown rice	5 ounces brown rice
1 kipper fillet (8 oz/225g)	1 kipper fillet (8 ounces)
1 small onion, chopped	1 small onion, chopped
Freshly ground black pepper	Freshly ground black pepper
Lemon juice	Lemon juice
1×10 oz (275g) tin broad beans	1×10 ounce can fava beans

1. Cook the rice in boiling salted water in a covered pan for approximately 20 minutes.

2. Cut the kipper into strips, add with onion to the rice.

3. Continue cooking until rice is tender and has absorbed all the water. Season with the pepper and lemon juice.

4. Heat the broad (fava) beans separately, drain and stir into the fish and rice mixture.

5. Serve with cooked frozen peas and grilled fresh tomatoes. *Do not freeze.*

Opposite: Quick and convenient and enough for two, Kipper Kedgeree (above). Single portion servings of Prawns in Nut Sauce (page 78) and Quick Beans (page 76).

Cauliflower Mince (MF)
'A quick and unusual midweek meal'

(Serves 2)

Total Fibre = 15g
Total Calories = 700
Total Carbohydrate = 40g
Each serving contains 20g CHO and 350 calories

Imperial (Metric)	American
8 oz (225g) lean minced beef	8 ounces lean ground beef
1 small onion, finely chopped	1 small onion, finely chopped
1 teaspoon Worcester sauce	1 teaspoon Worcester sauce
1 beef stock cube	1 beef stock cube
1×14 oz (400g) tin chopped tomatoes	1×14 ounce can chopped tomatoes
1 teaspoon tomato purée	1 teaspoon tomato paste
1 teaspoon mixed herbs	1 teaspoon mixed herbs
Sea salt	Sea salt
Freshly ground black pepper	Freshly ground black pepper
1 small (1 lb/450g) cauliflower, trimmed	1 small (1 pound) cauliflower, trimmed
¼ pint (150ml) skimmed milk	⅔ cup skimmed milk
1 oz (25g) fresh wholemeal breadcrumbs	½ cup fresh wholewheat breadcrumbs
1 oz (25g) reduced fat (15%) hard cheese, grated	1 ounce reduced fat (15%) hard cheese, grated
Paprika	Paprika

1. Brown the mince without added fat in a heavy-based ovenproof pan.

2. Drain off any fat. Add the onion, the Worcester sauce, crumble in the stock cube and stir in the tomatoes, tomato purée (paste), herbs and seasoning. Cover and simmer gently.

3. Meanwhile break the cauliflower into small pieces and cook until tender (but not mushy) in salted water. Drain very well and turn into a basin. Add the milk and breadcrumbs and beat well. Season with plenty of black pepper.

4. Remove the meat from the heat. Cover with the cauliflower mixture.

5. Sprinkle over the cheese and a little paprika. Grill or bake in a hot oven 400°F/200°C (Gas Mark 6) until brown and heated through.

6. Serve with broad (fava) beans or cooked frozen green peas and wholemeal granary rolls.

Spicy Shepherds Pie (MF)

(Serves 4)

Total Fibre = 30g
Total Calories = 1100
Total Carbohydrate = 140g
Each serving contains 35g CHO and 275 calories

Imperial (Metric)
1 lb (450g) potatoes, peeled
8 oz (225g) lean minced beef
1×15 oz (425g) tin borlotti beans
or 1×15 oz (425g) tin chick peas
Freshly ground black pepper
1 large onion, chopped
1 tablespoon tomato purée
1 small green pepper, diced
1 teaspoon chilli powder
¼ pint (150ml) beef stock
1×14 oz (400g) tin chopped
tomatoes

American
1 pound potatoes, peeled
8 ounces lean ground beef
1×15 ounce can pinto beans
or 1×15 ounce can garbanzo beans
Freshly ground black pepper
1 large onion, chopped
1 tablespoon tomato paste
1 small green pepper, diced
1 teaspoon chili powder
⅔ cup beef stock
1×14 ounce can chopped tomatoes

1. Cook the potatoes. When soft, drain and mash with black pepper and a little skimmed milk. Leave to cool.

2. Cook the mince in a heavy pan until browned. Remove with a draining spoon to a mixing bowl. Discard the fat.

3. Drain and rinse the tinned beans (or peas). Add to the mince and season with black pepper.

4. Simmer the onion, tomato purée (paste), pepper and chilli (chili) powder in the stock for 10 minutes until softened.

5. Pour onto the mince and beans. Add the chopped tomatoes. Mix well. Place in an ovenproof dish. Spread the potato over the meat. *Freeze at this point if desired.*

6. Cook at 400°F/200°C (Gas Mark 6).

Peachy Chicken (LF)

(Serves 2)

Total Fibre = 5g
Total Calories = 660
Total Carbohydrate = 50g
Each serving contains 25g CHO and 330 calories

Imperial (Metric)	**American**
2 small boned chicken breasts (12 oz/350g)	2 small boned (12 ounce total) chicken breasts
1 teaspoon paprika	1 teaspoon paprika
Sea salt	Sea salt
1 teaspoon sunflower oil	1 teaspoon sunflower oil
1×14½ oz (410g) tin peach slices in natural juice	1×14½ ounce can peach slices in natural juice
1 small onion, finely chopped	1 small onion, finely chopped
1 tablespoon arrowroot	1 tablespoon arrowroot
Freshly ground black pepper	Freshly ground black pepper

1. Season the chicken with the paprika and salt.

2. Heat the oil in a small non-stick pan, add the chicken, seal and cook for 2-3 minutes. Carefully transfer chicken to an ovenproof dish.

3. Add the peaches and most of the juice to the pan with the onion. Simmer for 2-3 minutes. Blend the arrowroot with the remaining juice and quickly stir into the pan.

4. Pour the peach mixture over the chicken. Season with plenty of pepper. Cover and cook in a pre-heated oven at 350°F/190°C (Gas Mark 5) for 30-40 minutes.

5. Serve with small jacket potatoes or boiled brown rice and mixed vegetables.

Fruit Caps (LF)

(Serves 4)

Total Fibre = 10g
Total Calories = 340
Total Carbohydrate = 40g
Each serving contains 10g CHO and 85 calories

Imperial (Metric)	**American**
1×14½ oz (410g) tin apricot or peach halves in fruit juice	1×14½ ounce can apricot or peach halves in fruit juice
2 large egg whites	2 large egg whites
2 tablespoons ground almonds	2 tablespoons ground almonds
2 tablespoons oatmeal	2 tablespoons oatmeal
2 teaspoons fruit sugar (fructose)	2 teaspoons fruit sugar (fructose)
½ teaspoon cinnamon	½ teaspoon cinnamon

1. Drain the fruit (reserve the juice to make a gelatine jelly with). Place the halves in a small ovenproof dish.

2. Whisk the egg whites until they form soft peaks.

3. Mix the almonds, oatmeal, fruit sugar and spice together.

4. Fold the almond mixture into the egg whites.

5. Spoon the meringue mixture into the fruit halves.

6. Bake in a pre-heated oven at 325°F/170°C (Gas Mark 3) for about 30 minutes, until the meringue is browned and crisp.

7. Serve hot or cold. *Do not freeze.*

Apple Batter (LF)

(Serves 6)

Total Fibre = 20g
Total Calories = 720
Total Carbohydrate = 90g
Each serving contains 15g CHO and 120 calories

Imperial (Metric)	**American**
1 lb (450g) eating apples, peeled and finely sliced	1 pound eating apples, peeled and finely sliced
1 oz (25g) desiccated coconut	⅓ cup desiccated coconut
1 tablespoon sunflower margarine, melted	1 tablespoon sunflower margarine, melted
¼ pint (150ml) skimmed milk	⅔ cup skimmed milk
2 oz (50g) wholemeal flour	½ cup wholewheat flour
1 size 3 egg	1 size 3 egg
½ teaspoon almond flavouring	½ teaspoon almond flavouring

1. Place the sliced apples in a 6-inch (15cm) ovenproof dish.

2. Sprinkle with half the coconut and brush over the melted margarine.

3. Whisk the milk, flour, egg and almond essence together.

4. Pour over the apple. Sprinkle with remaining coconut. Place in a pre-heated oven and bake at 375°F/190°C (Gas Mark 5) until browned and set — approximately 30 minutes.

5. Serve hot or cold as preferred. *Do not freeze.*

Muesli Meringue (LF)

(Serves 6)

Total Fibre = 20g
Total Calories = 360
Total Carbohydrate = 120g
Each serving contains 20g CHO and 60 calories

Imperial (Metric)	**American**
1×14½ oz (410g) tin apricot halves in juice	1×14½ ounce can apricot halves in juice
5 oz (150g) sugar-free muesli	1 cup sugar-free muesli
1 size 3 egg white	1 size 3 egg white
1 teaspoon fruit sugar (fructose)	1 teaspoon fruit sugar (fructose)

1. Drain the apricots, reserve the juice.

2. Mix muesli and juice together. Press the mixture into 6-inch (15cm) non-stick or lightly oiled sandwich tin.

3. Arrange the apricot halves, rounded side uppermost, over the mixture. Leave to stand for 10-15 minutes.

4. Bake in a pre-heated oven at 400°F/200°C (Gas Mark 6) for 15 minutes.

5. Meanwhile whisk the egg white until it forms soft peaks. Stir in the fruit sugar.

6. Remove the tin from the oven, reduce temperature to 350°F/180°C (Gas Mark 4).

7. Spread meringue over the centre of the fruit. Return to the oven until the meringue is browned. *Do not freeze.*

8. Serve warm or cold. Cut into 6 slices.

7.

NO-COOK COOKING

Russian Bulghur Starter (LF)
'An easy and economical use of salmon'

(Serves 6)

Total Fibre = 10g
Total Calories = 540
Total Carbohydrate = 60g
Each serving contains 10g CHO and 90 calories

Imperial (Metric)
3 oz (75g) bulghur (cracked wheat)
1×7½ oz (210g) tin red salmon,
  drained
2 tablespoons fresh lemon juice
Freshly ground black pepper
Iceberg lettuce, shredded
Garnish — 6 radishes, sliced

American
½ cup bulghur
1×7½ ounce can red salmon,
  drained
2 tablespoons fresh lemon juice
Freshly ground black pepper
Iceberg lettuce, shredded
Garnish — 6 radishes, sliced

1. Soak the bulghur in cold water for at least 2 hours. Drain well and leave to become completely dry on a piece of kitchen roll.

2. When the bulghur is dry, flake the salmon removing any obvious bone and skin.

3. Mix the bulghur, salmon and lemon juice together.

4. Season with plenty of freshly ground black pepper.

5. Line small bowls, sundae dishes or saucers with the shredded lettuce. Divide the bulghur mixture between the 6.

6. Garnish with the sliced radishes. *Do not freeze.*

Vegan Pâté (LF)

(Serves 8 large helpings)

Total Fibre = 20g
Total Calories = 480
Total Carbohydrate = 80g
Each serving contains 10g CHO and 60 calories

Imperial (Metric)
1 teaspoon *gelazone*
¼ pint (150ml) cold water
1×15½ oz (440g) tin chick peas
1×14 oz (400g) tin chopped
  tomatoes
3 oz (75g) fresh wholemeal
  breadcrumbs
1 clove of garlic, crushed
Freshly ground black pepper
¼ teaspoon sea salt

American
1 teaspoon vegetarian gelatine
⅔ cup cold water
1×15½ ounce can garbanzo beans
1×14 ounce can chopped tomatoes
1½ cups fresh wholewheat
  breadcrumbs
1 clove of garlic, crushed
Freshly ground black pepper
¼ teaspoon sea salt

1. Using a little of the water make a paste of the vegetarian gelatine. Stir into the remaining water. Bring to the boil whisking occasionally.

2. Drain and rinse the chick peas (garbanzo beans).

3. Place the chick peas, tomatoes, breadcrumbs, garlic and seasoning in a blender or processor.

4. Add the cooled gelatine mixture.

5. Blend or process to a smooth purée.

6. Turn into a serving dish and leave to firm or set. Garnish with black pepper.

7. Serve with fresh crudites or wholemeal toast fingers. *Do not freeze.*

Avocado Creams (LF)

(Serves 4)

Total Fibre = 5g
Total Calories = 480
Total Carbohydrate = 15g
Each serving contains negligible CHO and 120 calories

Imperial (Metric)	**American**
2 ripe avocados (8 oz/225g approx.)	2 ripe avocados (8 ounces approx.)
1 small onion, finely chopped	1 small onion, finely chopped
¼ pint (150ml) natural low-fat yogurt	⅔ cup natural low-fat yogurt
Juice of ½ lemon	Juice of ½ lemon
¼ teaspoon cayenne pepper	¼ teaspoon cayenne pepper

1. Peel and stone the avocados. Place in a blender or processor.

2. Add the onion, yogurt, lemon juice and cayenne pepper.

3. Blend or process to a smooth cream. *Freeze at this point if desired.*

4. Pour into 4 small individual pots. Chill.

5. Serve garnished with slivers of cucumber.

Coconut Cups (LF)

(Serves 6)

Total Fibre = 10g
Total Calories = 570
Total Carbohydrate = 15g
Each serving contains negligible CHO and 95 calories

Imperial (Metric)	**American**
2 size 3 eggs, separated	2 size 3 eggs, separated
½ pint (275ml) skimmed milk	1⅓ cups skimmed milk
½ teaspoon vanilla flavouring	½ teaspoon vanilla flavouring
6 tablespoons desiccated coconut	6 tablespoons desiccated coconut
2 teaspoons (1 sachet) gelatine	2 teaspoons gelatine
2 sachets non-nutritive sweetener	2 sachets non-nutritive sweetener

1. Over a low light (or over hot water), whisk the milk, egg yolks, vanilla flavouring and coconut together. Continue until the mixture starts to thicken. Remove from the heat.

2. Sprinkle on the gelatine, dissolve in the mixture. When cool, add the sweetener.

3. Whisk the egg whites until they form soft peaks. Gently fold into the custard.

4. Divide across 6 tulip shaped wine glasses and leave to set.

5. Serve garnished with a little toasted coconut.

6. *Do not freeze.*

Egg Pâté (LF)

(Serves 4)

Total Fibre = negligible
Total Calories = 160
Total Carbohydrate = negligible
Each serving contains negligible CHO and 40 calories

Imperial (Metric)	American
2 size 3 eggs, hard-boiled	2 size 3 eggs, hard-boiled
1 tablespoon skimmed milk	1 tablespoon skimmed milk
Pinch of paprika	Pinch of paprika
Freshly ground black pepper	Freshly ground black pepper
2 teaspoons red wine vinegar	2 teaspoons red wine vinegar
1 teaspoon tomato purée	1 teaspoon tomato paste
2 teaspoons Dijon mustard	2 teaspoons Dijon mustard

Garnish — parsley and cayenne
    pepper
	Garnish — parsley and cayenne
	    pepper

1. Place all the ingredients in a blender or processor.

2. Blend or process to a smooth paste (or pass through a sieve).

3. Spoon into individual ramekin dishes.

4. Chill for 2 hours before serving.

5. Garnish with parsley and cayenne pepper. *Do not freeze.*

Apricot Fool (MF)

(Serves 4)

Total Fibre = 25g
Total Calories = 360
Total Carbohydrate = 80g
Each serving contains 20g CHO and 90 calories

Imperial (Metric)
3 oz (75g) dried apricots, chopped
2 small peeled bananas (5 oz/150g)
⅓ pint (200g) low-fat natural yogurt
2-3 drops orange colouring
  (optional)
Garnish — sliced banana

American
3 ounces dried apricots, chopped
2 small peeled bananas (5 ounces)
¾ cup low-fat plain yogurt
2-3 drops orange colouring
  (optional)
Garnish — sliced banana

1. Poach the apricots in a little water until softened. Cool.

2. Put the apricots and their juice, bananas, yogurt and colouring in a blender or processor. Blend or process for a minute or two.

3. Divide between 4 small sundae dishes or wine glasses.

4. Chill in the fridge.

5. Serve garnished with sliced banana dipped in lemon juice. *Do not freeze.*

Cool Raspberry Mould (HF)
Illustrated opposite page 80.
(Serves 4)

Total Fibre = 50g
Total Calories = 200
Total Carbohydrate = 40g
Each serving contains 10g CHO and 50 calories

Imperial (Metric)
1½ lbs (675g) fresh or frozen
  raspberries
2 teaspoons gelatine (1 sachet)
¼ pint (150ml) buttermilk
Liquid or intense sweetener to taste

American
6 cups fresh or frozen raspberries
2 teaspoons gelatine
⅔ cup buttermilk
Liquid or intense sweetener to taste

1. Gently cook the raspberries without additional water in a covered pan until softened. Cool.

2. Dissolve the gelatine in a little water. Add to the raspberries. Leave until starting to set.

3. Stir in the buttermilk and sweetener. Whisk, blend or process to a smooth cream.

4. Divide equally between 4 small wine glasses or dessert bowls. Chill in fridge until set.

Prune Whip (LF)

(Serves 6)

Total Fibre = 25g
Total Calories = 660
Total Carbohydrate = 120g
Each serving contains 20g CHO and 110 calories

Imperial (Metric)	**American**
½ fresh lemon	½ fresh lemon
5 oz (150g) dried prunes	5 ounces whole dried prunes
½ pint (275ml) water	1⅓ cups water
3 oz (75g) dried dates, chopped	½ cup chopped dried dates
2 teaspoons (1 sachet) gelatine	2 teaspoons gelatine
¼ pint (150ml) evaporated milk	⅔ cup evaporated milk
2-3 drops vanilla flavouring	2-3 drops vanilla flavouring

1. Put the lemon, prunes and water in a pan. Bring to the boil, cover and simmer for 15 minutes. Remove from the heat and leave to stand for 1 hour.

2. Stone the prunes, place in a blender or processor.

3. Heat the prune liquor, add the dates and sprinkle on the gelatine. When dissolved remove from the heat and allow to cool.

4. Transfer to the blender or processor and mix to a smooth purée.

5. Whisk the evaporated milk until it starts to thicken, whisk into the purée mixture with the vanilla flavouring.

6. Transfer to a glass serving dish or individual sundae glasses. Serve with a garnish of natural yogurt.

Citrus Dessert (LF)

(Serves 4)

Total Fibre = negligible
Total Calories = 320
Total Carbohydrate = 10g
Each serving contains negligible CHO and 80 calories

Imperial (Metric)	**American**
2 lemons, washed	2 lemons, washed
1 large orange, washed	1 large orange, washed
½ pint (275ml) water	1⅓ cups water
2 tablespoons fruit sugar (fructose)	2 tablespoons fruit sugar (fructose)
2 teaspoons (1 sachet) gelatine	2 teaspoons gelatine
2 size 3 eggs, separated	2 size 3 eggs, separated
Orange colouring (optional)	Orange colouring (optional)

1. Remove the rind from the fruit and gently cook until tender in the water with the fruit sugar.

2. Squeeze the peeled fruit and strain into a small dish. Sprinkle over the gelatine and leave to stand.

3. Beat the egg yolks in a small basin. Add the strained fruit syrup. Heat the basin over water until the egg mixture thickens slightly.

4. Remove from heat, stir in juice and gelatine mixture, mix well. Leave until quite cold.

5. Whisk the egg whites until quite stiff, fold into the gelatine mixture. Add colour if desired.

6. Divide between 4 tall wine glasses or small sundae dishes.

7. Leave to set. Before serving garnish with chopped nuts or a few tangerine or mandarin segments. *Do not freeze.*

'Bitter' Cocktail Jelly (LF)

(Serves 4)

Total Fibre = negligible
Total Calories = 340
Total Carbohydrate = 60g
Each serving contains 15g CHO and 85 calories

Imperial (Metric)

1×14 oz (400g) tin fruit cocktail in
fruit juice
2 teaspoons (1 sachet) gelatine
¼ pint (150ml) sugar-free bitter
lemon
2-3 drops green food colouring
(optional)
Low/no-calorie sweetener to taste
1 tablespoon toasted coconut
4 oz (100g) black or green grapes,
halved

American

1×14 ounce can fruit cocktail in fruit
juice
2 teaspoons gelatine
⅔ cup sugar-free bitter lemon
2-3 drops green food colouring
(optional)
Low/no-calorie sweetener to taste
1 tablespoon toasted coconut
4 ounces black or green grapes,
halved

1. Turn the fruit cocktail into a pint (550ml) bowl or mould.

2. Dissolve the gelatine in a little water in the usual way.

3. When dissolved stir into the fruit cocktail.

4. Pour on the bitter lemon, mix well.

5. Colour and sweeten to taste.

6. Chill in a refrigerator until set.

7. Serve (turned out from the mould if used) decorated with the toasted coconut
    and halved grapes.

Weekday Trifle (LF)

(Serves 4)

Total Fibre = 5g
Total Calories = 600
Total Carbohydrate = 60g
Each serving contains 15g CHO and 150 calories

Imperial (Metric)	American
½ pint (275ml) skimmed milk	1⅓ cups skimmed milk
1 tablespoon custard powder	1 tablespoon custard powder
Liquid or non-nutritive powder sweetener to taste	Liquid or non-nutritive powder sweetener to taste
1×10½ oz (300g) tin mandarins in natural juice plus 2 slices pineapple with a little natural juice, chopped	1×10½ ounce can mandarins in natural juice plus 2 slices pineapple with a little natural juice, chopped
or 1×14½ oz (410g) tin fruit cocktail in fruit juice	*or* 1×14½ ounce can fruit cocktail in fruit juice
2 teaspoons (1 sachet) gelatine	2 teaspoons gelatine
Sugar-free squash or fizzy drink	Sugar-free squash or fizzy drink
Orange colouring (optional)	Orange colouring (optional)
¼ pint (150ml) single cream, whipped	⅔ cup light cream, whipped
Garnish — a little fruit reserved from the cans, toasted flaked nuts and toasted coconut	*Garnish* — a little fruit reserved from the cans, toasted flaked nuts and toasted coconut

1. Warm the milk, mix the custard powder to a paste with 1 tablespoon of water. Stir into the warmed milk and continue cooking, stirring continuously until it thickens. Leave to cool. Sweeten to taste.

2. While the custard is cooling, drain the fruit and turn into a deep glass bowl, reserve a little of the fruit for a garnish. Warm the reserved juice, sprinkle on the gelatine, stir until dissolved. Leave to cool in a measuring jug. When cool stir in enough strong sugar-free squash or fizzy drink to make up to ¾ pint. Pour over the fruit, sweeten to taste and leave to set (about 1 hour) in a cool place.

Opposite: Time for tea with Buttermilk Scones (page 104), Nut Macaroons (page 109), Fruit 'n Root Cake (page 101) and Pineapple Slice (page 98).

3. Stir occasionally to stop the fruit sinking to the bottom.

4. When the jelly is quite set pour over the custard, cover and leave in the fridge until ready to serve.

5. Then whip the cream until it is thickening and spread over the custard.

6. Garnish with the reserved fruit, toasted nuts and coconut. *Do not freeze.*

Ginger Fruit Salad (LF)

(Serves 4)

Total Fibre = 5g
Total Calories = 240
Total Carbohydrate = 60g
Each serving contains 15g CHO and 55 calories

Imperial (Metric)	**American**
1 large crisp apple, washed and sliced	1 large crisp apple, washed and sliced
1 small banana, peeled and sliced	1 small banana, peeled and sliced
1 tablespoon lemon juice	1 tablespoon lemon juice
1 small tin (10½ oz/300g) mandarin segments in natural juice	1 small can (10½ ounce) mandarin segments in natural juice
¼ pint (150ml) sugar-free American Ginger Ale	⅔ cup sugar-free American Ginger Ale
½ teaspoon ground ginger	½ teaspoon ground ginger

1. Place the apple, banana and lemon juice in the serving dish.

2. Add the can of mandarins and their juice, stir in the Ginger Ale.

3. Sprinkle over the ground ginger.

4. Cover and chill for at least 2 hours before serving. *Do not freeze.*

Opposite: Just right for friends, Kipper Pots (page 112), Oriental Rice (page 111) and Summer Cheesecake (page 120).

8.

SNACKS

Pineapple Slice (LF)
'A favourite snack'
Illustrated opposite page 96.
(Makes 8 slices)

Total Fibre = 15g
Total Calories = 880
Total Carbohydrate = 160g
Each slice contains 20g CHO and 110 calories

Imperial (Metric)	American
1×15 oz (425g) tin pineapple in natural juice	15 ounce can pineapple in natural juice
5 oz (150g) oats	1¼ cups oats
1 teaspoon cinnamon	1 teaspoon cinnamon
¼ pint (150ml) skimmed milk	⅔ cup skimmed milk

1. Chop (or process) the pineapple finely then turn into a mixing bowl. Add the retained juice, oats and spice. Mix well.

2. Pour on the milk. Stir. Cover and leave to stand for at least ½ hour. This softens the oats and gives the slice its 'gooey' texture.

3. Turn into a non-stick or lightly greased 7-inch (18cm) sandwich tin. Smooth the surface.

4. Bake in the top of the oven at 350°F/190°C (Gas Mark 5) for 1-1¼ hours until golden and set. The top will be crispy and the remainder light and spongy.

5. Allow to cool completely before turning out. *This freezes* but it is much too nice not to eat straight away!! Cuts into 8 good slices.

Carob Crunchy (LF)

(Makes 16 squares)

Total Fibre = 30g
Total Calories = 1600
Total Carbohydrate = 160g
Each square contains 10g CHO and 100 calories

Imperial (Metric)   **American**
3 oz (75g) sugar-free muesli   ¾ cup sugar-free muesli
3 oz (75g) self-raising wholemeal   ¾ cup self-raising wholewheat flour
  flour   ¾ cup rolled oats
3 oz (75g) rolled oats   ¼ cup wheat bran
1 oz (25g) wheat bran   2 tablespoons carob
2 tablespoons carob   2 tablespoons fruit sugar (fructose)
2 tablespoons fruit sugar (fructose)   ½ teaspoon baking soda
½ teaspoon bicarbonate of soda   1 teaspoon cream of tartar
1 teaspoon cream of tartar   2 teaspoons ground ginger
2 teaspoons ground ginger   5 ounces low-fat sunflower spread
5 oz (150g) low-fat sunflower spread

1. Mix all the dry ingredients together.

2. Rub in (or use a mixer) the low-fat spread, until the mixture is a stiff paste.

3. Transfer the mixture onto a non-stick or lightly oiled, swiss roll tin. Use a fork to spread the mixture, pressing down well.

4. Bake in a pre-heated oven 350°F/180°C (Gas Mark 4) for about 40 minutes when it should be firm and crisp.

5. While still warm cut into 16 squares and when quite cold transfer to container.

Economy Cake (LF)

(Makes 12 small slices)

Total Fibre = 25g
Total Calories = 1380
Total Carbohydrate = 180g
Each slice is 15g CHO and 115 calories

Imperial (Metric)	**American**
1 large cooking apple	1 large cooking apple
5 oz (150g) cooked potato	5 ounces cooked potato
2 oz (50g) dried, stoned dates	2 ounces dried, stoned dates
⅛ pint (75ml) English unsweetened apple juice	⅓ cup English unsweetened apple juice
5 oz (150g) self-raising wholemeal flour	1¼ cups self-raising wholewheat flour
1 teaspoon baking powder	1 teaspoon baking powder
2 teaspoons mixed spice	2 teaspoons mixed spice
2 oz (50g) sunflower margarine	¼ cup sunflower margarine
2 size 3 eggs	2 size 3 eggs

1. Peel and core the apple. Process or liquidize with the potato, dates and juice. Cover and set aside.

2. Mix the flour, baking powder and spice together. Rub in the margarine (or use a mixer or processor).

3. Add the apple mixture and the eggs. Beat well.

4. Turn into a non-stick or lightly oiled 7-inch cake tin.

5. Bake in a pre-heated oven at 350°F/180°C (Gas Mark 4) for about 1 hour 15 minutes until brown, risen and firm.

6. Cool on a cooling rack before cutting. *Do not freeze.*

Fruit 'n Root Cake (LF)
Illustrated opposite page 96.
(Makes 16 slices)

Total Fibre = 45g
Total Calories = 1440
Total Carbohydrate = 240g
Each slice contains 15g CHO and 90 calories

Imperial (Metric)	**American**
3 oz (75g) sultanas	½ cup golden seedless raisins
2 oz (50g) raisins	⅓ cup raisins
½ pint (275ml) hot tea	1⅓ cups hot tea
8 oz (225g) self-raising wholemeal flour	2 cups self-raising wholewheat flour
2 oz (50g) ground almonds	½ cup ground almonds
8 oz (225g) finely grated carrot	8 ounces finely grated carrot
1 size 3 egg	1 size 3 egg
1 teaspoon mixed spice	1 teaspoon mixed spice
1 teaspoon baking powder	1 teaspoon baking powder

1. Soak the dried fruit in the tea for as long as possible (overnight gives the best results).

2. Put the flour, almonds, carrot, egg and spice in the mixing bowl.

3. Add the fruit and tea mixture. Mix well. Stir in baking powder.

4. Turn into a non-stick or lightly oiled 2 pound (900g) cake or loaf tin.

5. Bake at 375°F/190°C (Gas Mark 5) for 1¼-1½ hours until firm and an inserted skewer comes out clean. Allow to cool before transferring to a cooling rack.

6. Cuts into 16 good slices.

Chocolate Swiss Roll (LF)

(Cuts into 10 slices)

Total Fibre = 20g
Total Calories = 1100
Total Carbohydrate = 150g
Each serving contains 15g CHO and 110 calories

Imperial (Metric)	**American**
2 tablespoons cocoa powder	2 tablespoons cocoa powder
⅛ pint skimmed milk	¼ cup skimmed milk
3 size 3 eggs	3 size 3 eggs
3 oz (75g) fruit sugar (fructose)	½ cup fruit sugar (fructose)
5 oz (150g) self-raising wholemeal flour	1¼ cups self-raising wholewheat flour
1 teaspoon baking powder	1 teaspoon baking powder
2 oz (50g) low-sugar high fruit jam	2 ounces low-sugar high fruit jam

1. Blend the cocoa and skimmed milk to a paste. Gently cook over a low heat for 2-3 minutes. Leave to cool.

2. Whisk the eggs and fruit sugar (use a mixer if possible) until the mixture is thick and forms a trail.

3. Stir in the cooled cocoa mixture.

4. Gently fold in the flour and baking powder. Mix well but not too vigorously.

5. Pour into a standard swiss-roll tin which is lined with oiled greaseproof paper.

6. Bake in a pre-heated oven at 425°F/220°C (Gas Mark 7) for about 20 minutes until brown, firm and risen.

7. Turn out on to greaseproof paper which is resting on a clean damp tea towel.

8. Spread with the jam (warm it if necessary).

9. Roll up immediately. Leave with the greaseproof paper holding the roll until quite cold.

10. Cuts into 10 slices.

Almond Tea Buns (LF)

(Makes 24 cakes)

Total Fibre = 35g
Total Calories = 1800
Total Carbohydrate = 120g
Each bun contains 5g CHO and 75 calories

Imperial (Metric)
2 oz (50g) dried apricots, finely
   chopped
5 oz (150g) self-raising wholemeal
   flour
3 oz (75g) ground almonds
1 teaspoon baking powder
3 tablespoons fruit sugar (fructose)
3 tablespoons sunflower oil
2 size 3 eggs, beaten
¼ pint (150ml) skimmed milk
A few drops almond essence

American
2 ounces dried apricots, chopped
1¼ cups self-raising wholewheat
   flour
¾ cup ground almonds
1 teaspoon baking powder
3 tablespoons fruit sugar (fructose)
3 tablespoons sunflower oil
2 size 3 eggs, beaten
⅔ cup skimmed milk
A few drops almond essence

1. Put the dry ingredients in the mixing bowl.

2. Add the oil, eggs and milk. Blend or beat well.

3. Stir in the almond essence.

4. Spoon the mixture into a non-stick or lightly oiled bun tin, making 24 buns
   in all.

5. Bake in a pre-heated oven at 400°F/200°C (Gas Mark 6) for about 15 minutes
   or until the buns are risen and springy to touch.

6. Allow to cool on a cooling rack before storing. *These freeze well.*

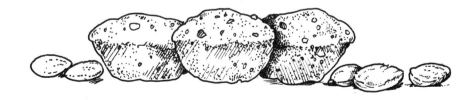

Buttermilk Scones (LF)

Illustrated opposite page 96.
(Makes 8 scones)

Total Fibre = 20g
Total Calories = 1280
Total Carbohydrate = 160g
Each scone contains 20g CHO and 160 calories

Imperial (Metric)	**American**
8 oz (225g) wholemeal flour	2 cups wholewheat flour
1 teaspoon baking powder	1 teaspoon baking powder
3 oz (75g) sunflower margarine	⅓ cup sunflower margarine
¼ pint (150ml) buttermilk	⅔ cup buttermilk

1. Place the flour and baking powder in a mixing bowl. Add the margarine. Rub in until mixture resembles breadcrumbs.

2. Pour in the buttermilk. Mix well, forming a soft dough.

3. Turn out onto a lightly floured board. Roll out a round ¾-inch (2cm) thick. Using a 2-2½-inch (5-6cm) cutter, cut out 8 scones.

4. Transfer to a non-stick or lightly oiled baking tray. Lightly brush with an egg and milk mixture.

5. Bake at 425°F/220°C (Gas Mark 7) for 15-20 minutes until brown and risen. They should sound hollow when the bottoms are tapped.

6. Transfer to a cooling rack. When cool, serve on their own or with savoury or sweet fillings. *These freeze well.*

Shortbread (LF)

(Makes 14 fingers)

Total Fibre = 20g
Total Calories = 1460
Total Carbohydrate = 140g
Each finger contains 10g CHO and 105 calories

Imperial (Metric)	**American**
5 oz (150g) wholemeal flour	1¼ cups wholewheat flour
1 oz (25g) brown rice flour	¼ cup brown rice flour
1 oz (25g) wholewheat semolina	¼ cup wholewheat semolina
¼ teaspoon sea salt	¼ teaspoon sea salt
3 oz (75g) sunflower margarine	⅓ cup sunflower margarine
2 oz (50g) fruit sugar (fructose)	⅓ cup fruit sugar (fructose)
½ teaspoon vanilla flavouring	½ teaspoon vanilla flavouring
1-2 tablespoons skimmed milk	1-2 tablespoons skimmed milk

1. Mix the two flours, semolina and salt.

2. Rub in (or use a mixer) the margarine. Stir in the fruit sugar, continue mixing until the mixture is sticking together.

3. Add the vanilla flavouring. Knead well.

4. Add the milk if the mixture is too dry and will not hold together.

5. Wrap in cling film and rest in fridge for 1 hour.

6. Knead again, form into 14 fingers and prick with a fork. (Easy method — roll out into a sausage, cut into 14 slices and shape each into fingers, lightly prick.)

7. Bake in a pre-heated oven at 325°F/170°C (Gas Mark 3) for about 20 minutes or until brown and crisp.

8. Cool on a cooling rack. *Freeze at this point if desired.*

Coconut Shortcake (LF)

(Makes 10 portions)

Total Fibre = 20g
Total Calories = 1150
Total Carbohydrate = 100g
Each piece contains 10g CHO and 115 calories

Imperial (Metric)	**American**
3 oz (75g) wholemeal flour	¾ cup wholewheat flour
1 oz (25g) self-raising wholemeal flour	¼ cup self-raising wholewheat flour
	¼ cup wholewheat semolina
1 oz (25g) wholewheat semolina	⅓ cup desiccated coconut
1 oz (25g) desiccated coconut	4 tablespoons fruit sugar (fructose)
4 tablespoons fruit sugar (fructose)	¼ cup sunflower margarine
2 oz (50g) sunflower margarine	Vanilla essence, a few drops
Vanilla essence, a few drops	

1. Mix all the dry ingredients together. Rub in the margarine (or use a mixer or processor).

2. Stir in the vanilla essence. Knead the mixture until it forms a soft ball.

3. Press into a round (6-inch/15cm diameter) non-stick baking dish.

4. Cover and leave in a cold place for about an hour.

5. Bake in a pre-heated oven at 350°F/180°C (Gas Mark 4) until brown and crisp — about 30-40 minutes. While warm make into 10 portions.

6. Turn out onto a cooling tray when quite cold. Cut into 10. *Freeze at this point if desired.*

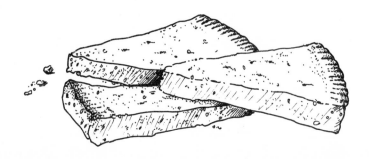

Oatcakes (LF)

(Makes 18 oatcakes)

Total Fibre = 20g
Total Calories = 1530
Total Carbohydrate = 180g
Each oatcake contains 10g CHO and 85 calories

Imperial (Metric)	**American**
5 oz (150g) oatmeal	1¼ cups oatmeal
3 oz (75g) wholemeal flour	¾ cup wholewheat flour
3 oz (75g) sunflower margarine	⅓ cup sunflower margarine
2 tablespoons sultanas, finely chopped	2 tablespoons golden seedless raisins, finely chopped
2 tablespoons fruit sugar (fructose)	2 tablespoons fruit sugar (fructose)
½ teaspoon mixed spice	½ teaspoon mixed spice
3-4 tablespoons skimmed milk	3-4 tablespoons skimmed milk

1. Mix the oatmeal and flour together. Rub in the margarine.

2. Add the sultanas (golden seedless raisins), fruit sugar and mixed spice. Mix well.

3. Add the milk and mix to a soft dough.

4. Turn out onto a floured surface. Roll to about ⅓ inch (⅔cm) thick.

5. Using a 2-inch (5cm) cutter, cut out 18 oatcakes.

6. Bake on non-stick or lightly oiled baking trays in a pre-heated oven at 350°F/180°C (Gas Mark 4) for about 40 minutes. The oatcakes should be brown and crisp. Cool on a cooling rack before *freezing* or transferring to an airproof biscuit tin.

Hazel Biscuits (LF)

(Makes 16 biscuits)

Total Fibre = 25g
Total Calories = 1760
Total Carbohydrate = 160g
Each biscuit contains 10g CHO and 110 calories

Imperial (Metric)	**American**
5 oz (150g) wholemeal flour	1¼ cups wholewheat flour
3 oz (75g) oatmeal	¾ cup oatmeal
3 oz (75g) hazelnuts, roasted, skinned and ground	⅔ cup hazelnuts, roasted, skinned and ground
3 oz (75g) sunflower margarine	⅓ cup sunflower margarine
4 teaspoons fruit sugar (fructose)	4 teaspoons fruit sugar (fructose)
1 teaspoon baking powder	1 teaspoon baking powder
1 size 3 egg, beaten	1 size 3 egg, beaten
1 teaspoon vanilla flavouring	1 teaspoon vanilla flavouring
Grated rind of 1 orange	Grated rind of 1 orange

1. Mix the flour, oatmeal and ground hazelnuts together.

2. Rub in the margarine.

3. Add the fruit sugar, baking powder, egg, vanilla and orange rind. Knead well. (Alternatively, mix all the ingredients using a food mixer until the mixture holds together.)

4. Divide into 16 balls. Flatten each onto a non-stick or lightly oiled baking tray.

5. Bake in a pre-heated oven at 375°F/190°C (Gas Mark 5) until brown and crisp — approximately 15-20 minutes.

6. Transfer to a cooling rack and allow to cool before placing in a biscuit/cake tin. *Do not freeze.*

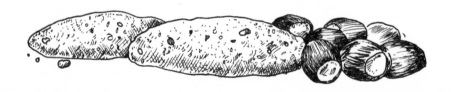

Nut Macaroons (LF)
Illustrated opposite page 96.
(Makes 20 Macaroons)

Total Fibre = 10g
Total Calories = 800
Total Carbohydrate = 30g
Each macaroon contains 1½ g CHO and 40 calories

Imperial (Metric)
5 oz (150g) hazelnuts or hazels and
   peanuts, ground
1 oz (25g) wholewheat semolina
2 tablespoons fruit sugar (fructose)
1 teaspoon cinnamon
2 egg whites, whisked
Rice paper
20 individual almond flakes

American
1 cup hazelnuts, ground
¼ cup wholewheat semolina
2 tablespoons fruit sugar (fructose)
1 teaspoon cinnamon
2 egg whites, whisked
Rice paper
20 individual almond flakes

1. Mix the ground nuts, semolina, fruit sugar and cinnamon together.

2. Stir in the stiff egg whites, mix gently.

3. Quickly spoon the mixture onto baking tray which has been lined with the
    rice paper, making 20 macaroons in all. Press an almond flake into each one.

4. Bake in a pre-heated oven 325°F/170°C (Gas Mark 3) for about 15 minutes
    or until brown and set.

5. They store well in an airtight container, but if frozen may need crisping in
    a hot oven or microwave.

9.

ENTERTAINING

Mackerel Dip (LF)

(Serves 10)

Total Fibre = 10g
Total Calories = 1100
Total Carbohydrate = 50g
Each serving contains 5g CHO and 110 calories

Imperial (Metric)
12 oz (350g) smoked mackerel,
  skinned
1×15 oz (425g) tin butter beans,
  drained
1 medium onion, chopped
1 teaspoon sunflower margarine
¼ pint (150ml) tomato juice
Freshly ground black pepper

American
12 ounces smoked mackerel,
  skinned
1×15 ounce can Lima beans, drained
1 medium onion, chopped
1 teaspoon sunflower margarine
⅔ cup tomato juice
Freshly ground black pepper

1. Process the mackerel and beans in a food processor or blend using a liquidizer.

2. Sweat the onions in a covered pan with the margarine.

3. Turn into the processor or liquidizer.

4. Add the tomato juice and black pepper.

5. Process or blend for a moment. *Freeze at this point if desired.*

6. Turn out into an attractive serving dish.

7. Garnish with lemon slices and watercress.

Oriental Rice (LF)

'A colourful and tasty party dish'
Illustrated opposite page 97.
(Serves 4 large or 8 small portions)

Total Fibre = 25g
Total Calories = 860
Total Carbohydrate = 160g
Each large serving contains 40g CHO and 215 calories

Imperial (Metric)	American
5 oz (150g) brown rice	5 ounces brown rice
1 teaspoon sunflower oil	1 teaspoon sunflower oil
1 medium red or green pepper, diced	1 medium red or green pepper, diced
1 medium onion, sliced	1 medium onion, sliced
8 oz (225g) bean sprouts	4 cups bean sprouts
2 tablespoons raisins	2 tablespoons raisins
¼ pint (150ml) unsweetened pineapple juice	⅔ cup unsweetened pineapple juice
2 teaspoons fruit sugar (fructose)	2 teaspoons fruit sugar (fructose)
3 oz (75g) tinned sweetcorn	½ cup canned sweetcorn
1 teaspoon soya sauce	1 teaspoon soy sauce
Garnish — chopped parsley, flaked almonds	Garnish — chopped parsley, flaked almonds

1. Boil the rice in salted water. Drain and rinse well.

2. Meanwhile heat the oil in a large frying pan (or wok). Add the peppers, onion and bean sprouts. Continue cooking until tender but still crisp.

3. Add the raisins, juice, fruit sugar, sweetcorn and soya (soy) sauce. Simmer for 5 minutes. Remove from heat.

4. When the rice is cooked and rinsed, combine with the vegetables and sauce. Mix well.

5. Serve hot or cold. Garnish with parsley and flaked almonds.

Kipper Pots (LF)

'Use dark well smoked kippers for the best results'
Illustrated opposite page 97.
(Serves 6)

Total Fibre = 5g
Total Calories = 360
Total Carbohydrate = 60g
Each serving contains 10g CHO and 60 calories

Imperial (Metric)	**American**
1 medium onion, finely chopped	1 medium onion, finely chopped
Small knob sunflower margarine	Small knob sunflower margarine
1 lb (450g) kipper fillets, skinned	1 pound kipper fillets, skinned
⅓ pint (200ml) water	¾ cup water
3 oz (75g) rolled oats	¾ cup rolled oats
Juice and chopped flesh of a large lemon	Juice and chopped flesh of a large lemon
Freshly ground black pepper	Freshly ground black pepper

1. Sweat the onions with the margarine in a covered heavy pan.

2. Cut the fillets into strips and poach in the water. When soft, remove from liquor. Discard any obvious bones. Liquidize or process.

3. Add the oats to the kipper liquid. Cook over a low heat until forming a thick sauce.

4. Turn into a bowl, add onions, kippers and lemon. Season and mix well.

5. Pile into six individual ovenproof non-stick or lightly oiled moulds or pots (3 inches/7.5cm). Smooth the surface. Place in a bain-marie. Cover the whole tray with foil.

6. Cook at 325°F/170°C (Gas Mark 3) for 20 minutes. Remove foil. Increase temperature to 375°F/190°C (Gas Mark 5) and continue cooking until browned. The mixture should have shrunk away from the sides of the mould slightly.

7. When cooled turn out onto individual plates of lettuce and tomato quarters. Garnish with lemon twists. *This freezes well.*

English Country Chicken (LF)

(Serves 4)

Total Fibre = 5g
Total Calories = 1100
Total Carbohydrate = 20g
Each serving contains 5g CHO and 295 calories

Imperial (Metric)	**American**
1 tablespoon sunflower oil	1 tablespoon sunflower oil
4 chicken portions (2 lbs/900g)	4 chicken portions (2 pounds)
1 large onion, chopped	1 large onion, chopped
8 oz (225g) celery, sliced	8 ounces celery, sliced
1 medium red pepper, sliced	1 medium red pepper, sliced
1 teaspoon dried thyme	1 teaspoon dried thyme
1 teaspoon dried sage	1 teaspoon dried sage
¼ pint (150ml) dry English wine	⅔ cup dry white wine
½ pint (275ml) tomato juice	1⅓ cups tomato juice
Freshly ground black pepper	Freshly ground black pepper
Sea salt	Sea salt

1. Heat the oil in a large heavy-based frying pan. Trim off any loose skin from the chicken portions and discard. Place the portions skin down in the pan. Cook for 5 minutes then turn and cook for a further 5 minutes. Transfer to plate.

2. Add the onion, celery, pepper, thyme and sage to the pan. Brown for 2-3 minutes.

3. Pour over the wine, cover and simmer for 5 minutes. Add the tomato juice and seasoning. Simmer for 2-3 minutes.

4. Place the chicken and the vegetable mixture in a large ovenproof casserole dish.

5. Cover and bake for 1½-2 hours at 375°F/190°C (Gas Mark 5). *Freeze at this point if desired.*

6. Serve with jacket potatoes, broccoli and sweetcorn.

Note: This is delicious if cooked on HIGH in a slow cooker for 5 hours.

Italian Lamb (LF)

(Serves 2)

Total Fibre = 5g
Total Calories = 480
Total Carbohydrate = 20g
Each serving contains 10g CHO and 240 calories

Imperial (Metric)	**American**
6 oz (175g) lean cubed lamb	6 ounces lean cubed lamb
Freshly ground black pepper	Freshly ground black pepper
Pinch of sea salt	Pinch of sea salt
1 teaspoon sunflower oil	1 teaspoon sunflower oil
1 medium onion, chopped	1 medium onion, chopped
1 clove of garlic, crushed	1 clove of garlic, crushed
2 fl oz (50ml) dry vermouth	¼ cup dry vermouth
1×14 oz (400g) tin chopped tomatoes	1×14 ounce can chopped tomatoes
4 oz (100g) mushrooms, sliced	4 ounces cup mushrooms, sliced
1 teaspoon Worcester sauce	1 teaspoon Worcester sauce

1. Mix the cubed lamb and seasoning together.

2. Heat the oil in a small heavy-based casserole.

3. Add the onion, garlic and seasoned meat.

4. Cover, reduce heat and continue heating until the meat is browned.

5. Remove cover, turn up heat and add the vermouth and mix well.

6. After a minute or two, add remaining ingredients.

7. Mix well. Cover and cook in a pre-heated oven for 45-60 minutes at 375°F/190°C (Gas Mark 5). Serve with jacket potatoes and broccoli or spring greens.

Party Pork (MF)

(Serves 6)

Total Fibre = 35g
Total Calories = 1590
Total Carbohydrate = 90g
Each serving contains 15g CHO and 265 calories

Imperial (Metric)	**American**
1½ lb (675g) lean pork	1½ pounds lean pork
Freshly ground black pepper	Freshly ground black pepper
¼ pint (150ml) white fruity wine	⅔ cup white fruity wine
1 large onion, finely chopped	1 large onion, finely chopped
Small knob of polyunsaturated margarine	Small knob of polyunsaturated margarine
2 tablespoons tomato purée	2 tablespoons tomato paste
2 tablespoons wholemeal flour	2 tablespoons wholewheat flour
½ pint (275ml) vegetable stock	1⅓ cups vegetable stock
3 oz (75g) aduki beans, soaked	3 ounces aduki beans, soaked
1 lb (450g) carrots, roughly chopped	1 pound carrots, roughly chopped
1 medium green pepper, cubed and blanched	1 medium green pepper, cubed and blanched
8 oz (225g) button mushrooms	8 ounces button mushrooms

1. Trim off any visible fat from the pork. Cut into small cubes. Season with plenty of the pepper.

2. Heat a heavy pan and add the pork. Maintain heat until the pork is sealed (and has lost all its pink colour). Reduce heat. Pour over wine and cover. Simmer for 5-10 minutes.

3. Meanwhile sweat the onions with the margarine in a heavy pan until transparent. Stir in tomato purée (paste), flour and stock.

4. Place the aduki beans, carrots, pepper and mushrooms in a pre-heated slow-cooker. Add the pork with its liquid. Pour over onion and stock mixture.

5. Cover and cook on HIGH for 6-8 hours. *This freezes well.*

6. Serve with jacket potatoes or wholemeal pittas.

Boozy Beef 'n' Prunes (MF)
'A rich and unusual dish'

(Serves 4)

Total Fibre = 30g
Total Calories = 1100
Total Carbohydrate = 80g
Each serving contains 20g CHO and 275 calories

Imperial (Metric)	American
1 lb (450g) lean braising beef, cubed	1 pound lean cooking beef, cubed
1 tablespoon wholemeal flour	1 tablespoon wholewheat flour
1 teaspoon horseradish mustard	1 teaspoon horseradish mustard
Freshly ground black pepper	Freshly ground black pepper
Sea salt	Sea salt
1 medium onion, chopped	1 medium onion, chopped
¼ pint (150ml) beef stock	⅔ cup beef stock
7 oz (200g) about 12-15 dried whole prunes	7 ounces dried whole prunes (about 12-15)
1×275ml can light ale	1⅓ cups canned light ale
1 tablespoon red wine vinegar	1 tablespoon red wine vinegar
1 oz (25g) wholemeal breadcrumbs	½ cup wholewheat breadcrumbs

1. Mix the cubed beef, flour, mustard and seasoning together. Turn into a heavy-based pan.

2. Place the pan on the heat, add the onion and stock, bring to the boil. Cover, reduce the heat and simmer for 5 minutes.

3. Add the prunes and light ale — bring to the boil. Remove from the heat.

4. Turn into the pre-heated slow-cooker. Add the vinegar and breadcrumbs. Cover and cook on HIGH for 5-6 hours or LOW for 8-10 hours.

5. *Freeze at this point if desired.*

6. Serve with whole green beans and jacket potatoes or creamed potatoes.

Fruit 'n' Seed Ice (LF)
'A unique mixture of tastes and textures'

(Serves 8)

Total Fibre = 20g
Total Calories = 1120
Total Carbohydrate = 160g
Each serving contains 20g CHO and 140 calories

Imperial (Metric)

3 oz (75g) dried stoned dates, chopped
3 oz (75g) fresh wholemeal or granary breadcrumbs
2 oz (50g) sunflower seeds, chopped
3 oz (75g) raisins
2 pub measures ($2 \times \frac{1}{6}$ gill/50ml) Tia Maria
½ pint (275ml) low-fat natural yogurt
Garnish — (optional) kiwi fruit, thinly sliced

American

½ cup dried, stoned, chopped dates
1½ cups fresh wholewheat breadcrumbs
2 ounces sunflower seeds, chopped
½ cup raisins
2 measures ($2 \times \frac{1}{6}$ gill) Tia Maria
1⅓ cups low-fat plain yogurt
Garnish — (optional) kiwi fruit, thinly sliced

1. Poach the dates in a little water until they form a soft paste. Add the breadcrumbs, sunflower seeds and raisins, cover and leave to cool.

2. Add the Tia Maria and gently stir in the yogurt.

3. Turn into a freezer-proof container and place in the freezer.

4. Remove the mixture before it freezes too solid (about 1-1½ hours). Beat well.

5. Turn out on to freezer foil — form into a roll and roll up into a roll (about 12 inches/30cm long). Return to freezer until frozen hard.

6. To serve, allow to soften slightly before cutting into 8 slices. Serve surrounded with sliced fruit — kiwi fruit looks superb, but mandarin segments or thinly sliced green skinned apple would do.

Strawberry Choux Ring (LF)

(Serves 8)

Total Fibre = 15g
Total Calories = 1080
Total Carbohydrate = 80g
Each serving contains 10g CHO and 135 calories

Choux Pastry:

Imperial (Metric)
¼ pint (150ml) water
2 oz (50g) sunflower margarine
3 oz (75g) wholemeal flour
2 size 3 eggs, beaten

American
⅔ cup water
¼ cup sunflower margarine
¾ cup wholewheat flour
2 size 3 eggs, beaten

Filling:

Imperial (Metric)
1×14 oz (400g) tin strawberries in juice
or approximately 1½ lb (675g) fresh or frozen strawberries, cooked in ⅛ pint (75ml) water
2 teaspoons (1 sachet) gelatine
1×8 oz (225g) carton skimmed milk (1% fat) cheese
2 sachets non-nutritive powder sweetener

American
1×14 ounce can strawberries in juice
or approximately 1½ pounds fresh or frozen strawberries, cooked in ¼ cup water
2 teaspoons gelatine
1×8 ounce carton skimmed milk (1% fat) cheese
2 sachets non-nutritive sweetener

1. Heat the water and margarine in a heavy-based pan. When the margarine has melted quickly whisk in the flour using a balloon whisk.

2. Continue heating gently and whisking or beating until the mixture forms a stiff paste.

3. Remove from the heat. Add the egg a little at a time, whisking well. When all the egg has been added continue whisking until the mixture is pliable and glossy.

4. Pipe or spread two-thirds of the mixture around a non-stick lightly oiled 8-inch (20cm) flan tin.

5. Using a teaspoon, spoon the remaining mixture into a non-stick lightly oiled 12-section bun tin.

6. Bake both in a pre-heated oven at 425°F/220°C (Gas Mark 7) for about 10-15 minutes. The ring and the little profiteroles should be well risen and crisp.

7. Turn the ring out onto a cooling tray, cut through horizontally and return to oven for 2-3 minutes to crisp the centre.

8. Cut the profiteroles and flap open, return to oven to crisp if necessary.

9. While the choux pastry is baking, drain the strawberries. Place the juice in a small pan, heat gently, sprinkle in the gelatine and allow to dissolve. Leave to cool.

10. When the juice is cooled transfer to a blender or processor, add the soft cheese, the drained fruit (reserving 6 small strawberries) and sweetener. Blend or process to a smooth purée. Leave until quite cool and setting.

11. Place the halved choux ring in an 8-9 inch (20-22cm) round glass dish. Spoon the strawberry mixture into the ring and into the centre. Replace the top ring.

12. Place half the strawberry in each profiterole. Pile onto the mixture in the centre.

13. Serve within an hour. *Do not freeze.*

Summer Cheesecake (LF)
Illustrated opposite page 97.
(Serves 6)

Total Fibre = 30g
Total Calories = 1280
Total Carbohydrate = 120g
Each serving contains 20g CHO and 210 calories

Flan Case:

Imperial (Metric)
3 oz (75g) low-fat sunflower spread
3 oz (75g) sugar-free muesli
3 oz (75g) self-raising wholemeal
   flour
2 tablespoons fruit sugar (fructose)
1 tablespoon ground almonds
1 teaspoon baking powder

American
¾ cup low-fat sunflower spread
¾ cup sugar-free muesli
¾ cup self-raising wholewheat flour
2 tablespoons fruit sugar (fructose)
1 tablespoon ground almonds
1 teaspoon baking powder

Filling:

Imperial (Metric)
8 oz (225g) fresh or frozen
raspberries or strawberries, washed
2 teaspoons *or* 1 sachet gelatine
1 pub measure ($\frac{1}{6}$ gill/24ml) Grand
Marnier
7 oz (200g) carton skimmed milk
(1% fat) soft cheese
Red colouring (optional)
Garnish — a little chopped nuts and
sliced raspberries or strawberries

American
2 cups fresh or frozen red soft fruit,
washed
2 teaspoons gelatine
1 measure ($\frac{1}{6}$ gill) Grand Marnier
7 ounce carton skimmed milk (1%
fat) soft cheese
Red colouring (optional)
Garnish — a little chopped nuts and
sliced raspberries or strawberries

1. Melt the sunflower spread over a low heat. Stir in the other ingredients.

2. Press into a fluted 6-7 inch (15-17cm) flan ring.

3. Bake in a pre-heated oven at 350°F/190°C (Gas Mark 5) until firm and brown.
    Allow to cool before removing flan ring. Transfer to the serving plate.

4. While the flan case is cooking, cook the soft fruit in a covered pan without
    added water. When soft, stir in the gelatine. Leave to cool.

5. Stir in the Grand Marnier and leave until starting to set.

6. Place cheese and fruit mixture in a blender and blend to a smooth cream. Add colour if desired. Leave until just starting to set again.

7. Spread over the flan case. Garnish with chopped nuts and sliced fruit.

Tropical Fruit (LF)

(Serves 6)

Total Fibre = 10g
Total Calories = 450
Total Carbohydrate = 90g
Each serving contains 15g CHO and 75 calories

Imperial (Metric)
1×14½ oz (411g) tin peach slices in juice
1 lb (450g) honeydew melon (about ½ a medium one)
1 large red-skinned apple, thinly sliced
1 medium banana, sliced
12 large deseeded and halved black grapes (3 oz/75g)
1 large juicy orange, peeled and sliced
¼ pint (150ml) cold water
2 pub measures (2×⅙ gill/50ml) white rum
Juice of a large lemon

American
1×14½ ounce can peaches in juice
1 pound honeydew melon
1 large red-skinned apple, thinly sliced
1 medium banana, sliced
12 large black grapes (3 ounces), deseeded and halved
1 large juicy orange, peeled and sliced
⅔ cup water
2 measures (2×⅙ gill) white rum
Juice of a large lemon

1. Turn peaches into a large serving dish.

2. Deseed and skin melon. Chop flesh roughly.

3. Add the melon, prepared apple, banana, grapes and orange to peaches.

4. Mix the water, rum and lemon juice together. Pour over fruit, mix well.

5. Cover and chill in fridge. *Do not freeze.*

6. Serve on its own or with wholemeal shortbread.

Lemon Dessert Flan (LF)

(Serves 8)

Total Fibre = 20g
Total Calories = 1520
Total Carbohydrate = 160g
Each serving contains 20g CHO and 190 calories

Flan Case:

Imperial (Metric)	American
3 oz (75g) sunflower margarine	⅓ cup sunflower margarine
3 oz (75g) rolled oats	¾ cup rolled oats
3 oz (75g) self-raising wholemeal flour	¾ cup self-raising wholewheat flour
1 teaspoon baking powder	1 teaspoon baking powder
2 oz (50g) fruit sugar (fructose)	2 ounces fruit sugar (fructose)

Filling:

Imperial (Metric)	American
1 tablespoon arrowroot	1 tablespoon arrowroot
Rind and juice of 2 lemons	Rind and juice of 2 lemons
2 oz (50g) sultanas	⅓ cup golden seedless raisins
¼ pint (150g) low-fat natural yogurt	⅔ cup low-fat plain yogurt
Few drops yellow colouring (optional)	Few drops yellow colouring (optional)
Decoration: lemon twists and a little toasted coconut	Decoration: lemon twists and a little toasted coconut

1. Place all the flan case ingredients in a heavy-based pan.

2. Gently heat until the margarine melts.

3. Press the ingredients together well.

4. Turn into a plain or fluted non-stick (or lightly oiled) flan ring or case — 6 inch (15cm).

5. Bake in a pre-heated oven at 375°F/190°C (Gas Mark 5) for approximately 20 minutes.

6. Allow to cool before transferring to serving plate.

7. While the base is baking, mix the arrowroot with the lemon rind and juice
    — place in a pan with the sultanas (golden seedless raisins).

8. Gently heat, stirring continuously.

9. As the mixture thickens, gently stir in the yogurt. Continue cooking for 2-3
    minutes. Stir in colouring (if required) at this point.

10. Remove from heat, continue stirring while cooling.

11. Spread the filling over the cooled base.

12. Before serving, decorate with lemon twists and the toasted coconut.

Appendix

THE CARBOHYDRATE AND CALORIE CONTENTS OF FOOD

The following list provides information on the approximate carbohydrate and calorie content of the foods featured in the recipes in this book. If you wish to omit or replace an ingredient in a recipe, remember to adjust the recipe calculation accordingly.

Figures are quoted per 100g and per lb (or oz) in weight. If you need to make changes in a recipe, remember to **SUBTRACT** the contribution of any ingredient you are omitting, from the **TOTAL CARBOHYDRATE** and **TOTAL CALORIE** figures for the recipe.

This will then be the figure for the amended recipe. If you are adding ingredients, to obtain the new calculation, remember to **ADD ON** their contribution to the stated figures. If you need to subtract **AND** add ingredients, you should do the subtraction **BEFORE** adding the contribution made by the additional ingredients.

Food	Approximate Carbohydrate Content		Approximate Calorie Content	
Almonds, ground	5g/100g	1.5g/oz	560/100g	160/oz
Almonds, flaked	5g/100g	1.5g/oz	560/100g	160/oz
Apple, cooking, fresh, whole	8g/100g	35g/lb	30/lb	140/lb
Apple, eating, fresh, whole	9g/100g	40g/lb	35/lb	160/lb
Apple juice, unsweetened	12g/100g	35g/½ pt	45/100ml	130/½ pt
Apricots, tinned in natural juice	40g/100g (14.5 oz) tin		190/410g (14.5 oz) tin	
Apricots, dried, stoned	43g/100g	12g/oz	180/100g	50/oz
Apricots, fresh whole	6g/100g	28g/lb	25/100g	125/lb
Arrowroot	95g/100g	27g/oz	360/100g	100/oz
Aubergine (Egg plant), fresh, whole	2g/100g	11/lb	10/100g	50/lb
Avocado pear, fresh whole	1g/100g	6g/lb	160/100g	720/lb
Bacon, lean, smoked, raw	—	—	150/100g	680/lb
Banana, fresh whole	11g/100g	50g/lb	50/100g	225/lb
Banana, fresh peeled	20g/100g	90g/lb	80/100g	360/lb
Beans, aduki, dried raw	35g/100g	10g/oz	230/100g	65/oz
Beans, barlotti dried, raw	45g/100g	12g/oz	270/100g	75/oz
Beans, barlotti, tinned	40g/425g (15 oz) tin		250/425g (15 oz) tin	
Beans, broad tinned	20g/290g (10 oz) tin		100/290g (10 oz) tin	
Beans, butter, dried, raw	50g/100g	14g/oz	270/100g	75/oz
Beans, butter, tinned	50g/425g (15 oz) tin		280/425g (15 oz) tin	
Beansprouts	3g/100g	10g/lb	15/100g	50/lb
Beef, lean, minced, raw	—	—	180/100g	800/lb
Beef, lean, stewing, raw	—	—	150/100g	680/lb
Blackberries, fresh or frozen, raw	6g/100g	30g/lb	30/100g	120/lb
Blackcurrants, fresh or frozen, raw	6g/100g	30g/lb	30/100g	120/lb
Breadcrumbs, fresh wholemeal	42g/100g	12/oz	220/100g	60/oz
Bran, wheat	20-25g/100g	5-7g/oz	175-200g/100g	50-60/oz
Brandy	—	—	220/100ml	60/fl oz
Bulghar (cracked wheat), dry	75g/100g	22g/oz	350/100g	100/oz

Food	Approximate Carbohydrate Content		Approximate Calorie Content	
Buttermilk	5g/150ml	5g/¼ pt	40/150ml	40/¼ pt
Cabbage, winter, raw	3g/100g	12g/lb	20/100g	100/lb
Cabbage, white, raw	3-4g/100g	15g/lb	20/100g	100/lb
Carob	10g/2 tablespoons		50/2 tablespoons	
Carrots, raw	5g/100g	20g/lb	20/100g	100/lb
Cauliflower, raw	1g/100g	5g/lb	10/100g	40/lb
Celery, fresh raw	1g/100g	5g/lb	5-10/100g	30/lb
Cheese, reduced fat (15%) hard	—	—	280/100g	80/oz
Cheese, full-fat, hard	—	—	400/100g	115/oz
Cheese, low fat (Quark) soft	negligible		90/100g	25/oz
Chicken, raw, boned	—	—	120/100g	540/lb
Chicken, raw, joints	—	—	90/100g	400/lb
Coconut, dessicated	6g/100g	1-2g/oz	600/100g	170/oz
Cocoa	8g/2 tablespoons		65/2 tablespoons	
Cod fillet, raw	—	—	70/100g	320/lb
Cornbeef, tinned	—	—	460/200g (7 oz) tin	
Courgettes, raw, whole	3g/100g	15g/lb	20/100g	100/lb
Cream, single	5g/150ml (¼ pt)		320/150ml (¼ pt)	
Cream, whipping	3-4g/150ml (¼ pt)		500/180ml (¼ pt)	
Custard powder	10g/1 tablespoon		35/1 tablespoon	
Dates, dried, stoned	65g/100g	18g/oz	250/100g	70/oz
Egg, raw whole size 3 (1)	—	—	75	
Egg, yolk raw size 3 (1)	—	—	65	
Egg, white raw size 3 (1)	—	—	10	
Flour, wholemeal, plain	66g/100g	300g/lb	320/100g	1440/lb
Flour, wholemeal, self-raising	66g/100g	300g/lb	320/100g	1440/lb
Flour, brown rice	75g/100g	34g/lb	350/100g	1575/lb
Fruit cocktail tinned in natural juice	50g/400g (14 oz) tin		190/400g (14 oz) tin	
Fruit sugar, fructose	100g/100g	30g/oz*	400/100g	115/oz

*NOTE: Usually ignored if less than 25g taken (less if other nutritive sweeteners eaten) in any one day.

Food	Approximate Carbohydrate Content		Approximate Calorie Content	
Gelatine	—	—	35/2 teaspoons (1 sachet)	
Grand Marnier	30g/100ml	7g/⅙ gill	280/100ml	70/⅙ gill
Grapes, black/green, fresh, whole	15g/100g	65g/lb	50/100g	225/lb
Herbs, dried or fresh	negligible		negligible	
Hazelnuts, shelled	6g/100g	2g/oz	380/100g	110/oz
Jam, low sugar, high fruit	30-35/100g	10g/oz	120/100g	35/oz
Kippers, fillets	—	—	205/100g	920/lb
Kiwi fruit, whole	6g/100g	27g/lb	35/100g	160/lb
Lamb, lean, boned, raw	—	—	160/100g	730/lb
Lamb, scrag end of neck, raw (1 lb when cooked with fat removed yields)	—	—	680	
Lemon, fresh (1)	—	—	10	
Lemon, juice from 1 large lemon	—	—	10	
Lentils, brown, green or red, raw	50g/100g	15g/oz	300/100g	85/oz
Lettuce, 1 large	—	—	15	
Liver, lambs, raw	—	—	180/100g	800/lb
Liver, pigs, raw	—	—	150/100g	690/lb
Mackerel, smoked fillet	—	—	215/100g	960/lb
Mandarins, tinned in natural juice	25g/300g (10½ oz) tin		100/300g (10½ oz) tin	
Margarine, sunflower	—	—	730/100g	210/oz
Melon, honeydew whole	3g/100g	13g/lb	10-15/100g	60/lb
Milk, evaporated	11g/100ml	3g/fl oz	160/100ml	45/fl oz
Milk, skimmed 1 pint	30g	—	190	
Milk, semi-skimmed 1 pint	30g	—	260	
Muesli, sugarfree	60-65g/100g	280g/lb	340-360/100g	1440-1600/lb
Mushrooms, whole raw	—	—	15/100g	70/lb
Mustard, 1 teaspoon	negligible		10	
Oats/Oatmeal, raw	73/100g	20g/oz	400/100g	110/oz
Oil, sunflower	—	—	900/100ml	255/fl oz
Onion, raw	5g/100g	25g/lb	20/100g	100/lb

Food	Approximate Carbohydrate Content		Approximate Calorie Content	
Orange, fresh, whole	6g/100g	30g/lb	25/100g	115/lb
Orange, seville, whole	5g/100g	25g/lb	20/100g	90/lb
Parsnip, whole, raw	8g/100g	40g/lb	35/100g	160/lb
Pasta, wholewheat macaroni, raw	65g/100g	19g/oz	330/100g	95/oz
Pasta, wholewheat shells, raw	65g/100g	19g/oz	330/100g	95/oz
Peas, chick, dried raw	50g/100g	14g/oz	320/100g	90/oz
Peas, chick, tinned	50g/440g (15 ½ oz) tin		320/440g (15 ½ oz) tin	
Peas, green, frozen	7g/100g	30g/lb	50/100g	225/lb
Peaches, tinned in natural juice	45g/410g (14 ½ oz) tin		180/410g (14 ½ oz) tin	
Peanut Butter, crunchy	20g/100g	5g/oz	580/100g	160/oz
Peppers, green or red whole	2g/100g	8g/lb	15/100g	60/lb
Pilchards, tinned in brine	—	—	500/425g (15 oz) tin	
Pineapple, tinned in natural juice	55g/425g (15 oz) tin		240/425g (15 oz) tin	
Pineapple juice, unsweetened	12g/100ml	35g/½ pt	45/100ml	130/½ pt
Pork, lean, minced, raw	—	—	150/100g	660/lb
Pork, lean, chops, raw	—	—	135/100g	600/lb
Pork, lean, stewing	—	—	150/100g	660/lb
Port, dry	3g/100ml	1.5g/⅓ gill	120/100ml	60/⅓ gill
Potatoes, cooked	20g/100g	90g/lb	80/100g	360/lb
Potatoes, raw	18g/100g	80g/lb	75/100g	340/lb
Prawns, shelled, cooked	—	—	110/100g	30/oz
Prawns, tinned in brine	—	—	175/200g (7 oz) tin	
Prunes, dried, whole	33g/100g	150g/lb	135/100g	600/lb
Raisins	64g/100g	18/oz	250/100g	70/oz
Raspberries, fresh or frozen	6g/100g	25g/lb	25/100g	110/lb
Rice, brown	72g/100g	20g/oz	350/100g	100/oz
Salmon, tinned	—	—	260/210g (7½ oz) tin	
Sauce Mix (casserole), 1 packet	30g		125	
Sausage meat, pork, raw	10g/100g	45g/lb	350/100g	1575/lb
Sesame seeds	20g/100g	5g/oz	560/100g	160/oz
Semolina, wholewheat	65g/100g	18g/oz	360/100g	100/oz
Spices	negligible		negligible	
Steak, minced	—	—	150/100g	675/lb
Stock, beef, 1 pint	negligible		15	
Stock, chicken, 1 pint	negligible		15	
Stock, fish, 1 pint	negligible		15	
Stock, vegetable, 1 pint	negligible		15	
Strawberries, fresh whole	6g/100g	27g/lb	25/100g	110/lb
Strawberries, tinned in natural juice	40g/400g (14 oz) tin		140/400g (14 oz) tin	
Sultanas	64g/100g	18g/oz	250/100g	70/oz
Sunflower seeds	20g/100g	5g/oz	560/100g	160/oz
Sunflower spread, low fat	—	—	350/100g	100/oz
Sweetcorn, canned	55g/330g (11½ oz) tin		250/330g (11½ oz) tin	
Tia Maria	30g/100ml	7g/⅙ gill	280/100ml	70/⅙ gill
Tofu, firm	9g/175g (6 oz) packet		160/175g (6 oz) packet	
Tomato Juice	3g/100ml	10g/½ pt	15/100ml	45/½ pt
Tomato purée (paste)	10g/100g	3g/oz	65/100g	20/oz
Tomatoes, tinned, chopped	10g/400g (14 oz) tin		50/400g (14 oz) tin	
Tomatoes, whole, raw	3g/100g	10g/lb	15/100g	60/lb
Tuna, tinned in brine	—	—	220/200g (7 oz) tin	
Vermouth, dry, white	2-3g/100ml	1.5g/⅓ gill	110/100ml	55/⅓ gill
Vermouth, rosso	15g/100ml	7g/⅓ gill	150/100ml	75/⅓ gill
Vinegar	negligible		negligible	
Watercress, 1 bunch	negligible		10	
Wine, white, dry	negligible		65/100ml	100/¼ pt
Wine, white, medium dry	3g/100ml	5g/¼ pt	75/100ml	120/¼ pt
Yogurt, natural low fat	10g/150g (5.3 oz) pot		80/150g (5.3 oz) pot	

INDEX